MAIN LIBRARY
STO

ACPL ITEM
DISCARDED

S0-BFQ-377

How To Promote
Yourself
Your Product
Your Service
or Your Organization
on Television

By
Wicke Chambers
and
Spring Asher

CHASE
communications

Allen County Public Library
Ft. Wayne, Indiana

Copyright © 1986 by Wicke Chambers and Spring Asher.

All rights reserved. No part of this book may be reproduced or
transmitted in any form or by any means, electronic or mechanical,
including photocopying, recording or by any information storage
and retrieval system, without permission from the authors.

Library of Congress Catalog Card Number: 85-73428

ISBN: 0-9615565-8-7 Hardcover
       0-9615565-9-5 Softcover

Published by Chase Communications, Inc.
     1776 Nancy Creek Bluff, N.W., Atlanta, GA 30327

Printed in the United States of America

Table of Contents

These are some of the people who made "Noonday" and this book possible.

Acknowledgements

Our special thanks to Cecil Walker, president and general manager of WXIA-TV, whose support of this project made it a reality.

Thanks to Jeff Davidson, former president and chief executive officer of Gannett Broadcasting Group, who made us part of the Gannett team.

And we are grateful to Alvin Flanagan, mentor of "11 Alive Noonday" and former president and general manager of WXIA-TV, who hired us to be the executive producers of the show and worked us until we "got it right. . . details, details, details."

We would never have "gotten it right" without Tracy Green and Ellen Berman, hardworking producers-extraordinaire, whose ideas and humor made "11 Alive Noonday" creative and energetic.

We are ever grateful to the "Noonday" family who were each a part of the whole that made "Noonday" exciting every day: hostess Yetta Levitt, director Jim Schoonmaker, technical director Gary Meadows, audio engineer Mel Weiss, videfont operator Collette Banks, camera people Evelyn Mims, Gordon Green and David Maschinot.

Thanks also to news producer Billy Otwell, anchors Andrea Nissen, Dave Michaels, Joe Washington and loveable weatherman Guy Sharpe. A special thanks to artist L.J. Morin and to cameramen Lowell Bailey, Al Ashe and David Brooks whose good eye made beautiful visuals for "Noonday" and to editors Birnur Richardson, Elliott Sparks, Wayne Clark and Jack Sanders.

Thanks also to special friends Mike Martin, Dave Howell, Bob Crawford, Pam Anderson, Dude King, Katherine Barker, Martha Hamilton and the voice of WXIA-TV, Ann Shelton.

Foreword

As broadcasters our responsibility is to present news, information and entertainment to the viewers. As the industry has developed, the viewer has become more sophisticated. The broadcaster and the viewer have grown to expect a more professional presentation of our product.

No longer would we be satisfied just to see John Cameron Swayze sit and read *about* the news. Now the reporter and cameraperson are there, *live on the scene,* showing us events and asking questions viewers want answered.

Jeff Davidson, former President, CEO and innovative leader of Gannett Broadcasting Group.

Television presents the news of the world, local politics, current events and public concerns. The viewer also wants lifestyle consumer information, the latest medical breakthrough, entertainment, fashion and business news. The resource for much of that is the publicist, convincing the television producer that a new long-wearing contact lens will be of interest to the viewer or that a new book will help viewers adapt to retirement. Each year over a million people appear as guests on talk shows and news programs presenting products, services and ideas that will inform and interest viewers.

Gannett's *USA TODAY* is quoted in this book as saying that 75 percent of the information in a newspaper is public relations generated. It is not true in television.

Our time is more limited, and our need for visual material and the ability of the guest to present an idea with authority requires more effort on the part of a person attempting to present a concept for television.

The television viewer expects a professional presentation, and the producer looks for that ability in a guest. Talk and news-feature producers are presenting consumer news to the viewer, and that news hook is what makes the subject an interesting choice for the show.

Wicke Chambers and Spring Asher are producers who take a creative approach to introducing new products and ideas to television. With this they can solve the problem of how to bring the best to television.

Jeff Davidson
Former President &
Chief Executive Officer
Gannett Broadcasting Group

Introduction

If you didn't see it on TV, did it really happen?

Television is the most exciting visual means for communicating information and entertainment in the 20th century. It outstrips all other mass media. Because of the combination of words, pictures, colors, music, animation, sound effects and immediacy, it offers unmeasured potency. There are more television sets in the U.S. than indoor toilets.

According to mass communications expert Marshall McLuhan, electronic communication dominates the lives of all Western people. It has replaced the age of print, and today it is the principal way men acquire knowledge and share it with others.

As television producers, we have been part of this exciting medium for more than 10 years. Our "11 Alive Noonday" show is an hour-long, noon news/talk show in Atlanta, the 16th major TV market in the country. As executive producers for this program, we found it important to "televisionize" each guest. That meant taking advantage of guests with demonstrations, pictures, videotapes, slides, anything visual that would allow our viewers to "see" as well as hear what was happening in the world today.

Over the years we have gotten calls with guest pitches from national and local PR firms, individuals, celebrity representatives, trade associations and financial experts who wanted to promote their fashions, diets, books, computers, errand services or church bazaars. Our message to them was always the same: "How can we best showcase your idea for television?"

To be part of an exciting industry, you have to be exciting. We hope in this book to use our experiences on "Noonday" to highlight the good guests and the innovative approaches to bookings to help you get your product, service or self on the screen with substance and sizzle.

The Power of Television

Part of the learning process about television is to understand the power of this medium. *Broadcasting Magazine* observes that after doctors and dentists, most Americans acquire health information from television. Dr. Timothy Johnson and Dr. Art Ulene offer health and medical information to millions regularly on the morning network programs.

Between 50-80 percent of Americans get their news information from TV. Because of its visual delivery of information, people are free to learn while they exercise, dress, work, eat, clean house or diaper a baby. They can watch the Super Bowl on the beach and see a space walk at the office. They can experience the visual joy of a royal wedding or the intimate sadness of a presidential funeral while at shopping malls or in a company lunchroom. Television makes you an eyewitness to international, national and local events.

Presenting Information

The Age of Communication is here and it is creating a new urgency about the way we present information, products and ideas to the public. This is where you come in. Knowing the latest television techniques gives you power to better utilize the medium for your message.

U.S. News and World Report published a 1984 report on "The World of Communications Wonder." In it they stated that "by the end of the century electronic information technology will have transformed American business, manufacturing, school, family, political and home life."

Presenting information about your company, your organization or yourself on TV can develop awareness, personalize your message, create visual impact and establish your credibility. Just ask us or the man, or woman, who's done it.

There are hundreds of books about how to break into print or how to write a press release, but we think that for the man with a message for television, we can offer you the best information on how to sell yourself to the electronic medium.

Hundreds of celebrities and ordinary people appear daily on news shows, public affairs programs or talk shows like "Noonday" to promote their product, service, cause or company. They have gained free promotion because they have a timely message that is unique or in some way enhances the viewers' lives. As award-winning television producers, we are experts on what television wants, what it can do for you, how to make contacts, how to create unique and interesting TV segments and news features, how to create visuals and how to become a memorable guest or interviewee.

We not only have booked over 400 celebrities, including Charlton Heston, Lou Rawls, Gloria Steinem, Oscar de la Renta, Alex Hailey, Rich Little, Christie Hefner, and Miss U.S.A., and ordinary people such as a veterinarian-turned-cookie-gram entrepreneur and a local potter, we ourselves have been booked as authors on national TV shows including "Good Morning America" and "Hour Magazine." Personally and professionally we know and understand the problems of getting booked on TV.

The purpose of this book is to give you media moxie. We know that it is good business to take your business to TV. It is our business to help you get there.

Wicke Chambers
Spring Asher

You Can't Sell 'Em If You Don't Tell 'Em!

Variety is the spice of "Noonday." Guests on one day included dancer Tommy Tune, Good Housekeeping Institute's Krestin McNutt, local real estate expert Joan Briener and Purina's pet pal, actress Betty Thomas.

What's the quickest way to make 100,000 or more house calls and let people know you're in business?

If you've started a business, written a book, created an original fashion design, developed a unique financial service, or work for a company that has started a new fitness program, or if you're a doctor or lawyer with something unique to sell or interesting to tell, you need to be on TV.

Six hundred thousand new businesses were created in the U.S. in 1983, and as any successful business person will tell you, "You can't sell 'em if you don't tell 'em." Competition is the name of the game, and if you want to create awareness and inform the public about your product, service, cause or yourself, you need to be on TV.

The Information Age

People want to know what's going on in the world. They want to know how to improve their lives without being overwhelmed with complicated advice or difficult techniques. If you can make their lives easier, more comfortable or more fulfilling, you need to be on TV.

Television is the most pervasive and influential medium. Superstar Jane Fonda said, "I used to be an elitist and look down on TV. Then I saw 'Roots' and the remarkable impact it had. You can't ignore TV. You've got to join it if you're interested at all in communicating." If *you're* interested in communicating your cause or company, you need to be on TV.

In this chapter we'll discuss the importance of television exposure, the difference between free publicity and paid advertising, how much media is available, whether you need a publicist or a public relations firm to get booked on television or whether you can do it yourself.

What Free Television Exposure Can Do for You

Establish Personal Contact

Television is the most personal of all media. You can establish eye contact and a one-to-one relationship with the audience. Viewers get a sense of the kind of person you are, what kind of personality you have and whether or not they can communicate with you. Personalized communication exerts a stronger influence on potential clients than a print piece.

Prince Charles's valet, Stephen Barry, is not a stodgy English butler. He is a man with charm and wit. Getting to know him as a person on TV made you more interested in buying and reading his books, *Royal Secrets* and *Royal Service.*

Create Awareness

TV/PR creates an awareness of your service or product. You may be known in your industry or organization, but TV allows you to make anywhere from 10,000 to several million house calls about your product or service in 4 minutes or less to a mass audience. TV is a visual showcase.

Dr. Ronald Goldstein is a cosmetic dentist well known in his field. After his TV appearances, he became well known to the masses.

Develop Sales Support

Using television as an effective communications tool establishes a sense of leadership. Management that takes its message to a mass medium is perceived as dynamic and progressive. Creating awareness of a product or service on television gives the company's sales staff an advantage and support when talking to clients. Often the client will say, "Oh, yes, I saw something about that on TV."

Flori Roberts, president of Dermablend, a corrective cosmetic for skin discoloration and disfigurement, took her product to TV. She demonstrated her product on port wine birthmarks and other skin disorders. Her TV appearance caused a surge at the cosmetic counter at Macy's department store after the program.

You Can't Sell 'Em If You Don't Tell 'Em!

Enhance Credibility

Television exposure gives you credibility. Your appearance signifies you have achieved some form of recognition for your work or your cause and creates a perception of credibility with your present clients and with the ones you hope to get. Unlike paid advertising, a TV appearance is a third-person endorsement.

An "emerging" business appeared more "established" after one of the partners appeared on TV. Barbara Baxt of Beadazzles, a shop that sells unique materials for creating high-fashion necklaces, became well known to fashion-conscious bargain hunters as well as prospective franchisees after her TV demonstration.

Create Free Publicity

Television reaches the largest audience at an extremely low cost. It is an effective way to communicate your message to potential customers or clients with no additional expense to them. A 4-minute interview on a local program is the equivalent of eight 30-second paid commercials.

The Computer Home Search Service introduced on TV its product designed to help home-buyers find homes in their preferred price and style bracket. Viewers were given inexpensive consumer information in an entertaining format.

Generate Public Response

TV appearances generate response. An enthusiastic fitness expert with a well thought-out running program had over 100 new applicants sign up in 1 hour on the day he was interviewed on our show.

A news story on a new amusement park that focused on possibilities of summer employment in the park generated enough calls to jam the park switchboard for hours after it appeared. The tape shown of the park in full swing generated customers who wanted to take part in the fun.

On a national level, an author's appearance on the "Phil Donahue Show" is said to generate as many as 40,000 sales of his book.

Produce Media Crossover Responses

Television appearances develop crossover possibilities for interviews with other media. Fitness experts, make-up artists or computer specialists who have appeared on television have an easier time selling their message to newspapers, magazines, industry journals or other TV programs. If you've appeared on television, it is more likely other programs will be interested in interviewing you.

Dr. Wayne Dyer, the author of *Your Erroneous Zones,* traveled across the country in a van promoting his first book on TV, radio, newspaper or whatever medium he could talk his way into. His cross-country effort created so much awareness for his book that it not only began to sell out, but to climb to the top of the charts of the bestseller list. His latest books have always been on the New York Times Best-Seller List. "You can't sell 'em if you don't tell 'em."

If you become a regular guest or expert on a TV program, you will soon become a "recognizable personality." Chef/author Julia Childs and Dr. Ruth Westheimer were professionals in their fields before becoming TV regulars and media personalities. Viewers develop a comfortable confidence and seek the advice of "Noonday's" TV lawyer, gardener or chef when they see one of them in public. They often call the station for their office numbers. "Regulars" develop an enthusiastic and loyal following, and although they usually start as informational news or consumer consultants, they often end up on the payroll. Unlike the aura of a "larger than life" movie star, TV regulars develop a "my friend" feeling among viewers. Viewers see our Dr. Andy Morley on the street and say, "Hi, Dr. Andy."

In the case of Andy Morley, there is no doubt that his reputation on TV led in part to his being chosen president of the Georgia Academy of Family Physicians. We at "Noonday" felt paternally proud to see him quoted on the front page of *The New York Times in* April 1985.

The Difference Between Paid Commercials and Free Publicity

Advertising is a paid message sponsored by a company. Publicity is any information or feature used, without cost, by the media because of its newsworthiness.

Advertising costs. News and feature air time is free. Advertising is limited by the amount of time you can afford to buy. Unique news and feature stories that will interest or serve the viewer offer unlimited opportunities for television air time.

A Clairol beauty product commercial costs thousands of dollars to produce and additional thousands to market on television. The Clairol Loving Care Scholarship, a program which offers scholarships up to $1,000 a year to women 30 or over who want to return to school, generates tremendous publicity at minimum expense each year. The company gains publicity when it announces the availability of the scholarships in the media and again when it announces the winners, all women over 30 who are the prime targets of their products. The viewer is impressed with the Loving Care attitude of the company, and the prospect of enhancing a viewer's life makes it an easy pitch to producers.

Advertising Advantage

Control of copy
Control of size of ad or length of TV time
Control of placement on TV or on print page
Control of artwork or photography
*But *you* pay for the privilege of such control.

Free Publicity Advantage

Third-party endorsement
Adds legitimacy to the product, service or cause.

The movie "Ghostbusters" was promoted heavily through advertising, but the free publicity generated by the term "ghostbusters" and the "ghostbusters" symbol kept the movie on the minds of more than just the moviegoers. The "ghostbusters" term created multiple adaptations from the judicial system's "crimebusters" to the soft drink industry's "thirstbusters."
Ciba Soft Color Lens makes television commercials to sell its product. Ciba gets free television time to demonstrate personal stories of how these lenses have changed the lives of models, make-up artists or ordinary people.

In order to interest a producer in your segment, you must be creative. You must convince him/her that your idea is newsworthy, timely, unique or is something that will enhance the life of the viewer. A producer's first consideration is the viewer. Will the viewer be interested, entertained or informed by this idea? That is the bottom line.

The Importance of Being Newsworthy

Being newsworthy is the key to your success. "When a dog bites a man, that is not news. When a man bites a dog, that is news." This adage is certainly true in the news room. When publicity seekers call the news room with a hyped-up story, a product promotion with little substance or viewer interest like the opening of an apartment complex, the general retort is "Take out an ad." Creating a segment that generates free advertising must have substance and must offer solid, interesting information presented in a unique manner. Doing your homework and having your information well packaged is the trade-off for getting free time.

Our station did a news feature on a service that videotapes household possessions for insurance purposes. This promotional piece was aired during a period when several house break-ins were being reported on the news.

A podiatrist who called to talk about foot ailments was rejected because he didn't really have an interesting hook. Another podiatrist called who wanted to talk about sport shoes and to explain which sport shoe to wear for which sport. Sports are always a hot topic, and running and aerobics events were in the news. He gave a successful talk and used interesting visuals in his demonstration.

9

JULY

Sun.	Mon.	Tues.	Wed.	Thur.	Fri.	Sat.
		1	2	3	4	5
6	7	8	9	10	11	12
13	14	15	16	17	18	19
20	21	22	23	24	25	26
27	28	29	30	31		

Producers' calendars are often packed from September to December. TV shows need guests Christmas week, holidays and summers. You can fill this need.

Being timely is an important element in getting free publicity. The months from September through November are always packed on TV calendars. But television shows *need* guests on the Fourth of July, Christmas week, Memorial Day or during the month of July. You might have much better success if you try for a spot during one of the slower times. It will give you the experience and exposure that will lead to future appearances.

Kenneth Goldwasser, a young gemologist just starting in the business of sales and appraisals, came on our show during a slow period to explain how to choose a diamond. He had a lot of good visuals, did a good job and offered to be available whenever we needed a stand-in guest. He parlayed his "TV experience" on our show into a newspaper article and an appearance on "P.M. Magazine."

An author who had written a religiously inspired book on her husband's battle with cancer was fighting a tough battle herself trying to get on television. She won her battle by tying the "miracle" of her husband's cure to the "miracle" of the Easter season and presented a timely segment on the Friday before Easter.

Another woman who had just started an errand service offered to pick up cans of food from merchants and individuals to support our station's big Thanksgiving Can-A-Thon Drive to feed the poor. Her appearance on TV was a timely segment for a community event and her business.

A nutritionist used the week before Halloween to demonstrate sugar-free snacks. A gift-wrapping service called offering unique ideas just before Christmas. A Bible company called with a segment about the variety of Bibles just before Easter, the biggest Bible season of all. Timing is everything in some cases. It may be in yours.

Being unique is also important. There are dozens of soaps on the market, but each manufacturer positions its advertising message to show its most unique or distinctive quality. One soap "wakes you up in the morning" while another one "gently caresses your body." Take a tip from the soaps and show why you're different, unique.

There are many people with ideas for making money, but author Robert G. Allen talks about making money in the real estate market in his book *Nothing Down*. No down payment—that's unique.

There are many people who start new businesses, but at 70 Jerome Schulman developed a new toothpaste that solves gum problems. He sold his product to more than 700 Chicago drugstores and was outselling mint-flavored Crest. His age, his success, his energy—that's unique.

Ann Oliver's business of offering a manners and grooming program to teens in this blue-jean society was so unique that she appeared on "Good Morning" and "P.M. Magazine" and in *Newsweek*.

Being the "first," the "youngest," the "only" helps to create free publicity. Many cooking or fitness experts are booked on TV because their diet is "quick" or their exercise program produces the "firmest" results.

Everyone wants to live better, more easily or less expensively. If you have an idea that will enhance the health, wealth or happiness of the viewer, you can sell it to a producer.

The following suggestions may spark creative ideas to help you get your product or service on television.

An auto mechanic offered to give money-saving tips on how to communicate with a mechanic or what to look for when buying a used car.

You Can't Sell 'Em If You Don't Tell 'Em!

Viva La Difference

Seventy-year-old entrepreneur Jerome Shulman developed a toothpaste to aid gum problems. His age, energy and success made him unique.

Viewer Enhancement

*Celebrity Punky Brewster lends
her support to P.R.I.D.E.,
Parents Resource Institute for
Drug Education.*

A restaurant owner who specialized in take-out foods presented 10 easy ways to have an instant dinner party.

A banker took her lead from the current Social Security developments in the news to offer senior citizens tips on banking and saving.

An interior decorator offered affordable ideas for fix-ups with paint and came again on Valentine's to give a timely segment on how to make your house romantic with lighting.

If you are creative, your idea does much of the work of selling your pitch to a harried producer. Your effort makes the producer look good, and you have developed a contact who will be interested in working with you in the future.

Many non-profit organizations vie for the limited amount of television time. One way to gain the attention of a producer is to involve a celebrity who will appear on behalf of your cause. This is also good exposure for the celebrity.

Singer Juice Newton promotes the National Kidney Foundation. It is her way of giving something back to the community and to the people who have supported her and her records.

Steve Lundquist, a Georgia resident and Olympic gold-medal swimmer, lends his support and his "celebrity" status to promote the autistic children's campaign in his home state. His name and his involvement create immediate awareness of the needs of these children.

Talent agents listed in the Yellow Pages can provide information on which celebrities might be available or interested in helping to promote charitable causes. Organizations can often save transportation expenses by holding their event close to a locally scheduled appearance a celebrity has already planned to make.

You Can't Sell 'Em If You Don't Tell 'Em!

The Star Connection

Olympic gold medal swimmer Steve Lundquist adds celebrity status to the Autism Services of Georgia in his hometown.

Many industries or trade associations use energetic personalities to act as their spokespersons and promote their products by going on media tours. These spokespersons offer how-to demonstrations, send-ins or ideas that help the viewer to live better by using their product.

ScotTowel, Jr. hired an efficiency expert to give time-saver tips, several of which utilized the new shorter-width, more efficient and economical ScotTowel, Jr. The company offered information that was of immediate benefit to the viewer and that created awareness for its new product.

Dow Chemical paid an exercise expert to create an exercise routine that could be done while you cleaned the bathroom. She also offered a free booklet describing the exercise routine. It was written and published by Dow Chemical. This is a bonus idea that gave the company a chance to promote its product while offering better-living tips.

Clairol sent a fashion expert to talk shows who demonstrated versatile fashion changes for travel. She included Clairol hair spray in her suitcase and used it in the quick-change demonstration.

If you are an enthusiastic cook, craft person or make-up artist or have some other expertise and are a relaxed, effective speaker, you may be able to "sell" your talent to a company and become their paid expert. Many business or trade associations, such as the wool industry or a financial association, use this method of getting time and promotion on talk shows and pay experts to travel and demonstrate their product.

Get some practice on your local television station. Make a tape of your appearance. Present the idea to a company that could be your "TV partner."

If you have the opportunity to tour, as a spokesperson for a product or as an author, be aware that it is tiring both mentally and physically. Consider this and do not overbook. Allow breathing and travel time between appearances.

Major cities now offer media escort services. This is helpful because your guide knows the city, can "find a parking space" and can even do your grocery shopping if you're touring as a chef. For information, contact *Pro-Motion: A Quarterly Newsletter for the Media Escort Network*, 17915 Shaker Blvd., Cleveland, Ohio 44120; (216) 295-1158.

How Much Media Is Available?

Think big. Television is a giant industry with a tremendous number of possibilities for TV bookings.

There are more than 600 network affiliate stations, 250 independent television stations, 290 PBS member stations and 70 stations with religious formats in the country.

The cable industry now has over 5,800 operating systems that broadcast on a 24-hour basis. Each of these stations has its own news, talk or public affairs programs that need newsworthy information to fill their air. Thirty or 60-minute formats are a fixed commodity and no matter what the problem—a guest who gets sick, a satellite transmission that doesn't come through or a tape with technical problems—there is still the same amount of time to fill. It might as well be with you.

People are out there watching. Ninety-eight percent of all homes have at least one television set, and that set is used more than 6 hours daily. TV households with cable rose from 39 percent to 44 percent in 1983. Seven million people watch the "Today" show nationally, and 164,000 households watch a 6:00 p.m. local news program in Atlanta, Georgia, daily.

Public libraries have books listing the names of the television stations and programs across the nation. Some of the best books which list news, talk or public affairs programs are:

All-In-One Directory
Gebbie Press, Inc.
Box 1000
New Paltz, NY 12561
Phone: (914) 255-7560

Covers basic information on over 22,000 publicity outlets in daily newspapers, weekly newspapers, radio and television stations. Price: $58 payment with order; $65 plus $2 handling when billed.

All TV Publicity Outlets Nationwide
Public Relations Plus, Inc.
Box 1197
New Milford, CT 06776
Phone: (203) 354-9361

Lists over 3,500 cable and broadcast programs that use outside guests, films or scripts. Gives contact's name and brief description of program. Price: $149.50 plus shipping and handling.

Broadcasting/Cablecasting Yearbook
Broadcasting Publications, Inc.
1735 DeSales Street, N.W.
Washington, DC 20036
Phone: (202) 638-1022

All television and radio stations and cable television systems in the United States and Canada. Price: $75.

Burrelle's Media Directories
75 East Northfield Avenue
Livingston, NJ 07039
Phone: (201) 992-7070

Offers three separate directories listing broadcast and print media that service black, Hispanic and women's special interest groups. Price: $35 for one volume, $65 for two volumes and $90 for all three volumes.

Directory of Religious Broadcasting
National Religious Broadcasters
Box 1926
Morristown, NJ 07960
Phone: (201) 428-5400

Covers about 4,000 radio and television stations, cable networks and others concerned with religious broadcasting. Price: $29.00 postpaid.

International Radio and Television Society-Roster Yearbook
International Radio and Television Society
420 Lexington Avenue
New York, NY 10170
Phone: (212) 867-6650

Lists 1,800 professionals involved in television or radio. Price: $15 for non-members.

People in Public Telecommunications
National Association of Educational Broadcasters
1346 Connecticut Avenue, N.W.
Washington, DC 20036
Phone: (202) 785-1100

Covers 500 public television and over 3,000 individuals in public education broadcasting. Includes national telecommunication agencies with staff listings. Price: $10.

Radio-TV Contact Service Cards
Media News Keys
40-20 27th Street
Long Island City, NY 11101
Phone: (718) 937-3990

Offers 3×5 cards that list radio and television programs (both local and network) that use guests and originate in the New York area. Price: $35.

Radio-Television News Directors Association Directory
Radio-Television News Directors Association
1735 DeSales Street, N.W.
Washington, DC 20036
Phone: (202) 737-8657

Lists over 2,000 U.S. and Canadian news directors. Available to members only.

Television Contacts
Larimi Communications
246 West 38th Street
New York, NY 10018
Phone: (212) 819-9310

Covers about 900 television stations, networks and syndicates interested in guests or outside scripts. Price: $159 including monthly updates.

TV News
Larimi Communications
246 West 38th Street
New York, NY 10018
Phone: (212) 819-9310

Covers about 750 local television news departments and about 150 national and regional network news programs and their staffs. Price: $119.

You Can't Sell 'Em If You Don't Tell 'Em!

Video Register
National Federation of Local Cable Programming
906 Pennsylvania Avenue S.E.
Washington, DC 20003
Phone: (202) 544-7277

Directory lists over 850 contacts for local cable programming. Price: $50 for non-members.

Working Press of The Nation
National Research Bureau
310 S. Michigan Ave.
Suite 1150
Chicago, IL 60604
Phone: (312) 663-5580

Separate volumes cover syndicates, 6,000 daily and weekly newspapers, 8,000 radio and television stations, and nearly 5,000 magazines. Price: complete set $250 or $115 for each of the five volumes.

Do You Need a Publicist or a Public Relations Firm to Get Booked on TV?

You might be surprised at the numbers and types of people you see on TV who use a PR firm to get there. Plastic surgeons, religious leaders, Girl Scout officials, hospital administrators, labor union leaders, singers, authors and dentists are just a few who do. Katharine Hepburn is reported to be the only star who has never had a publicist.

What Do PR Firms Do for Their Clients?

Public relations firms know the importance of getting their clients' names or products before the public. PR firms offer expert counseling. They evaluate clients' goals, target their audience and discuss the budgets necessary to reach these objectives. Some firms specialize in certain areas such as corporations, finance and investments, beauty and fashion, food and beverage, home furnishings, medicine or travel.

PR firms employ many experts, researchers, writers and artists to carry out these goals. They employ ex-reporters and news producers who have media contacts and backgrounds in different areas of television writing or producing. Having been on the receiving end of many press releases, they can bring clear, well-executed information to the media. These pros have a sense of what the media is interested in, who would be interested and how to contact that person.

Large PR firms offer a variety of personnel and services. They have account supervisors who design strategy, discuss long-range promotional programs, handle finances and oversee account executives.

Account executives handle the daily responsibilities of one or two large accounts and several smaller ones. They create slides or product shots for media kits and handle the drafting, writing, editing and proofing of media materials and biographical information. They match stories to contacts, call contacts and mail information. They can also set up video training sessions for clients before an on-camera appearance, handle logistics of clients' appearances or make arrangements for out-of-town clients. They monitor press, videotape TV appearances and handle the day-to-day responsibilities of their accounts.

Public relations firms come in all sizes. The largest may be international in scope and have several thousand employees. Then again there are many successful one-person local publicists who may be just the right size for your needs and your pocketbook.

The services of some of these larger firms don't come cheap. Many of the larger firms have monthly

You Can't Sell 'Em If You Don't Tell 'Em!

The Size and Fees of PR Firms

21

retainer fees that run over $6,000 for some clients. Even medium-size firms can have monthly charges as high as $4,000.

PR firms have a variety of billing procedures. Some bill by the hour, others by the month. Some charge a fee plus expenses, others offer an all-inclusive service. Some firms keep time sheets, and others charge a commission on out-of-pocket expenses.

PR Firms in Action

PR firms can operate as part of a company's internal structure or be hired as an outside independent service. The following are examples of how a corporate PR firm, an independent firm and a small one-person firm handle their clients.

Large Independent PR Firm

Hill and Knowlton, Inc., one of the large international PR firms, had a client in the cognac industry. Lifestyle facts in their media kit pointed out how cognac was no longer just for "royalty." It was definitely a "comer." Americans were eating better and cooking more at home, and in a recent nationwide cooking competition, 40 percent of the 1,000 recipes sent in used liqueurs. They suggested using an expert who could demonstrate a delicious dessert recipe for those who wanted to give an inexpensive dish a little dash. It was an informative and visually interesting segment for television.

An In-House PR Division

Rich's is a large department store chain that handles its own promotion. They know the local programs suitable for their clients and offer tremendous support and follow-through for any segment they book.

When actress Jane Powell was promoting a line of petite fashions for women, Rich's put together a lively "show and tell." They chose the clothes, selected the models and sent a media kit which included such facts as "not only was Jane Powell a petite size, under 5′4″, but so are 'big' stars such as Elizabeth Taylor, Joan Collins, and Bo Derek." This segment offered visual, interesting information with a "star."

A One-Person PR Firm

Karen Wantuck has a small one-person PR office. She has limited resources but a good eye for newsworthy TV stories. One of her clients opened the first gelato, an Italian ice shop, in her city.

She called offering highlights on the history of gelato, information on the low sugar and fat content and a list of the amazing variety of fresh flavors the shop offered.

She suggested giving a demonstration of the machine the owner used to make "spaghetti" gelato. The machine pushed the gelato through a dozen or more holes that made the ice cream come out in strands like spaghetti. Strawberry jam was used as the sauce and coconut sprinkles were used as a "cheese" spread over the top. The audience was entertained and informed, the crew loved it and the gelato shop got a huge response.

*How Do You Choose
a PR Firm?*

If you think a PR firm is necessary to get the job done for you, do your homework first. It is important to know the expertise of the firm, its best media contacts, its success quotient, its fee policies and billing procedures. Ask friends and associates for recommendations. Demand a straightforward answer from the firm about how marketable you or your product will be. Discuss timetables. Get a statement in writing about the services you are buying. Be sure you understand fees, expenses and add-on charges in advance.

A good PR firm or agent can be a good investment, but shop wisely.

Major corporations and trade associations know the importance of getting their name and products before the public. They use PR firms to keep their names and products on the consumer's mind.

Can you handle this job yourself? Certainly nobody knows the benefits, strengths and attention-getting qualities of your product, service or idea better than you. If you have enough imagination to create a product or service, you certainly have the ability to create good, newsworthy ideas for TV and can handle the job of establishing media contacts on your own. Patience, determination and salesmanship have big pay-offs. The following are a few good examples of people who were successful on their own.

Successful Self-Promoters

*A Self-Promoter with
Interesting Visuals*

Betty Harrison wrote *The Garage Sale Handbook.* She was an enthusiastic salesperson on the phone and talked about how giving tips on garage sales could help viewers get rid of their "treasures" and pick up extra cash in the process. She gave convincing arguments for getting over timidity and embarrassment when putting on a sale and stressed how important it was to include *every* unwanted item. Old make-up, broken appliances, unwanted kitchen items, even an extra set of false teeth can be a delight for handymen, bargain shoppers or curiosity seekers.

Betty appeared twice, once showing a wild assortment of odd and interesting items she had included in her sales. Another time she gave examples of effective garage sale signs. She was enthusiastic and timely and knew how to relate her message to the audience.

*A Self-Promoter with
a Good Story*

Jerome Schulman, another self-promoter, began his call with a most captivating opening: "I'm 71 years old, and I've created a toothpaste that has caused a revolution." He went on to say that he had been written up in *The Wall Street Journal* and *Advertising Age* (facts which helped to establish his credentials) for developing a toothpaste that not only helped his tooth and gum problems but also those of other people who had tried his product. He had letters of endorsement and an article which stated that in the 700 drug and food outlets in Chicago that carried his product, it outsold mint-flavored Crest. He was so convincing that we changed the calendar and got him on the program the next day.

*A Self-Promoter
with Determination*

Claire Costales handles her own promotion like a pro. As a recovered alcoholic and an author on the subject, she had made between 18-20 phone calls to the nationally syndicated TV show "Hour Magazine" to convince them to do a segment on her book. Never willing to give up easily, she ran up a powerful phone bill while she stirred up a dynamic amount of interest in her subject. Citing current statistics that 1 out of 4 Americans is touched in some way by alcoholism and doing a remarkable selling job, she landed a spot on a national TV show as a complete unknown. She talked about how co-workers and families touched by alcoholism could learn to deal personally with the problem and get help for themselves.

The day before her segment appeared nationally, she called to tell us about her appearance and to talk about scheduling a local follow-up segment on the same subject.

25

*Claire Costales, recovering
alcoholic and author who does
her own promotion, landed a
spot on "Hour Magazine."*

Having already attracted national attention, she found it was much easier to schedule a local appearance. This confident woman gave our viewers excellent information. She excited so much response, we rescheduled her for additional segments.

Good openers, good statistics, unique stories, newsworthy ideas, informative and helpful hints for viewers are effective sales techniques for any enthusiastic and organized person trying to get booked on television.

You've got what it takes, so go for it. The following chapters offer a step-by-step guide for helping you get your product, service, cause or self booked on TV.

When you decide to take your message to the electronic media, you need to go like a pro—prepared. As Bill Curry, Georgia Tech football coach, says, "Anyone can have the will to win, but do you have the will to *prepare*?"

In the next chapter Chambers & Asher demonstrate how to make a media kit that will take you to the tube.

Bump—What do Jeanne Dixon, Famous Amos and Lily Tomlin have in common? (Reveal). . . They all send media kits.

*A bump is a device used in TV to tease the next segment.

You Can't Sell 'Em If You Don't Tell 'Em!

Coming Up Next

The Media Kit

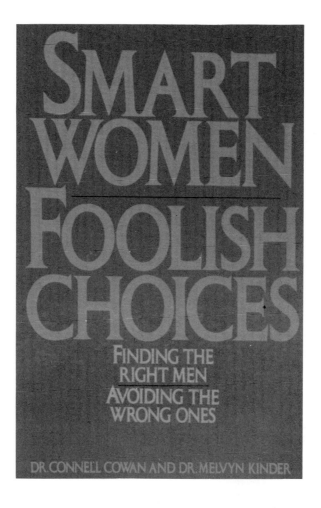

An effective media kit is a standard-size folder which contains carefully prepared information. A picture or book jacket will enhance the cover.

How do you package your information so that your substance has sizzle?

A media kit is the first step in exciting and interesting the media in your subject. It is basically a folder that contains the necessary information about yourself, your product, service or cause. Putting together a media kit helps you to

- organize your information and materials
- tell your story in a creative and unique way
- make the work of a harried producer easier.

A well-packaged media kit also allows you to cast about for nibbles of interest from producers or news departments. They may even call to request more information or to schedule appearances. This rarely happens, however. A good media package always includes follow-up phone calls.

Most media kits today seem to have been designed when print was king. The information included is usually pages of information that companies or individuals send out to 800 to 1,000 newspapers in hopes of getting some or all of it into print. After more than 30 years of operation, TV stations are still swamped with newspaper-style releases.

Today media kits for electronic journalism should have a fresh approach. This is the age of pictorial journalism. Information about the availability of pictures, slides, tapes or demonstrations should accompany standard facts and figures. Basic facts-and-figure information is still essential, but TV doesn't reproduce copy. It creates visual segments that are newsworthy and of interest or consequence to the viewer. Good visuals often get a story accepted when a straight presentation fails.

Effective media kits can be as easy and inexpensive as a folder from the drugstore or as expensive and elaborate as a glossy, 4-color package with printed inserts. Both are

The Media Kit

Media kit with photo of potential guest.

The Look of a Media Kit

designed to keep all of your materials together.

Your name, address and telephone number should be on *every* piece of paper. The papers inside the folder may be color-coordinated. Be neat, and remember *spelling counts!* Type double-spaced with wide margins. Don't send an outrageous-size folder to try to get attention. It will get away from the producer's stack of materials and get lost.

Be prepared to send the folder again if it gets lost. (Embarrassing, but true, they do get lost. There are many shows at each station, hundreds of guests and several producers who are changing jobs.) Carry a kit with you when you arrive for an appearance. Some stations are more prepared for you than others!

The Basic Media Kit

A good media kit has 2 purposes: to entice and to inform. The cover letter should hook the reader with brief, newsworthy comments. The fact sheet or background page should provide enough pertinent information for the reporter or host to ask knowledgeable, informed questions. Develop your kit with all of the information necessary to create interest and make a sale, but don't repeat facts. It is time-consuming to read the same information on every page. The complete kit contains the following:

- a cover letter
- a biography of the guest
- the fact sheet
- background information
- suggested questions
- clippings from print media
- a photograph or horizontal slide
- visuals (pictures, slides, props, videotape, models, etc.)
- the product, if it is a book, or picture, if a computer or make-up kit

- (optional) a list of shows the spokesperson has appeared on or an itinerary for his/her media tour.

The cover letter introduces the producer or assignment editor to the subject of the proposed media appearance. Media people get from 5 to 25 media kits a day, so this letter should be concise and use plenty of white space.

In this 1-page letter there should be 4 short paragraphs. The opening sentence or lead should get the reader's attention and motivate him to read on.
- Go for a fast opening punch—"One out of every 4 Americans is affected by alcoholism."
- Ask a question—"Did you ever think bankers were dull?"
- Use an imaginative dialogue lead-in—"He asked, 'Why did you decide to write a book about regaining your virginity?' She answered, 'It just seemed like a question that was on so many people's minds during this sexual revolution.'"

In this first paragraph you should hype the product, service or personality and back it up with good, solid facts. This paragraph explains the benefits to the viewer.
- This skin preparation is the first in its field to _____.
- It's a plan to relieve economic stress by _____.
- This product will make you "sexy" because _____.
- You can conquer your cholesterol problem with _____.
- Relate your information to current headlines. If you state that *The Wall Street Journal, Time,* and *Vogue* are all talking about Penny Stocks, it will reinforce the fact that the subject is newsworthy.

The second paragraph gives brief biographical information on the spokesperson:
- the editor of Penny Stock Newsletter
- the doctor who developed the permanent eyeliner
- the star in town on behalf of a cause.

The Media Kit

Cover Letter

PUBLIC RELATIONS

A horizontal slide can be used to promote a coming TV guest.

Fleishman-Hillard, Inc.
Public Relations
One Memorial Drive • St. Louis, Missouri 63102 • 314/982-1700 • TWX 910-761-1108

Kristine R. Brill
Account Executive

September 17, 1984

Spring Asher
"Noon Day"
WXIA-TV
1611 West Peachtree, N.E.
Atlanta, GA 30309

Dear Spring:

Lindsay Wagner's was peaceful. Dom Deluise's was fiesty and Tony Geary's was nearly deaf. That's the inside story on a few celebrities' cats from prize-winning animal photographer Bob Bishop.

Bishop knows all about celebrities and their cats. He just finished photographing the feline friends of 25 well-known stars for the 1985 Purina Cat Chow Celebrity Cats Calendar.

"Cats are more difficult to photograph than any other animal," says Bishop, "and capturing celebrities' cats on camera was especially challenging."

Bishop went on location to the homes of the participating cats and celebrities in order to utilize the natural environment. Each calendar photo features the celebrity cat surrounded by artifacts associated with its owner-star. In addition, a quote from each celebrity about his or her cat, along with the star's signature, appears adjacent to the photo.

When photographing cats, Bishop employs a bag full of tricks to gain the animal's attention. Cat toys, yarn, birds, crickets and mice are excellent attention-getters. Finger-snapping, barking and hissing work well, too.

Still, Bishop claims that patience is the key. "We had to reshoot the cover cats, Kenny and Marianne Rogers' kitties, 'Kit' and 'Kaboodle,' several times before we got perfect results," he says.

Bishop plans on visiting Atlanta on Wednesday, October 17, and would be available to share his tips on photographing cats and his inside stories on the celebrities and their cats. We can furnish color slides of each celebrities' cat and Bishop has even volunteered to demonstrate his talents with a live cat, if you'd like to see an actual photo session in action.

This cover letter is short and opens with attention-getting celebrity connection.

34

In the third paragraph tell how and why the audience will be entertained or informed. The audience will enjoy hearing about wine tasting because

- there will be an interesting demonstration on cooking with wine
- it is a chance to get a glimpse of "the world of the rich," those who buy a $15,000 bottle of wine
- it is a chance to learn how and when to serve different wines
- it is a chance to interview an entertaining expert.

The fourth paragraph gives a description of the possible visuals that are available:

- a tape on a California vineyard
- photos of wine processing
- a demonstration showing a variety of wine glasses
- historical photos of wines as seen in famous paintings.

Finally, tell the date of the prospective media appearance and give information concerning a related seminar, autographing or special event being held locally that the viewer might be interested in attending. If the date of the appearance is flexible, be sure to mention it. You will be better able to negotiate a scheduled appearance. Indicate that you will call soon to arrange for a media appearance.

This 1-page story gives the credibility of the "expert," the organization he represents and the position he holds. The "bio" can also give the person's motivation for becoming an expert spokesperson.

Give any information that shows that the expert has solutions to problems. Example: Tom Anderson has been in the air-conditioning business for 20 years, and his experience shows there are many things the viewer can do to prevent damage to air-conditioners.

Give information the viewer will find interesting. For

The Media Kit

A standard-size kit with a gimmick.

Biography of the Spokesperson

```
From:  Joan Carris
       Richard Weiner, Inc.
       888 Seventh Ave., N.Y. 10106
       (212) 315-8092

For:   Pecos Valley Spice Company


FACT SHEET FOR BROADCASTERS, EDITORS

WHO:              Jane Butel:
                  Nationally recognized authority on Tex-Mex and
                  Santa Fe regional cooking.

                  Founder and president of the Pecos Valley
                  Spice Company (manufacturers of pure,
                  authentic chiles, seasonings and ingredients
                  for Southwest regional cooking).

                  Author of six cookbooks, including "Jane
                  Butel's Tex-Mex Cookbook," "Chili Madness,"
                  "Finger Lickin', Rib Stickin' Great Tastin'
                  Hot and Spicy Barbecue" and "Woman's Day Book
                  of New Mexican Cooking."

WHAT:             Jane will conduct chili tasting at Davison's.

                  She will feature chili with all the fixin's
                  and Mixin's.

                  Friday, October 19
                  12 Noon - 3:00 P.M.
                  Davison's (downtown)
                  180 Peachtree Street, NW
                  Atlanta, GA

                  Saturday, October 20
                  12 Noon - 4:00 P.M.
                  Davison's
                  Lenox Square Mall
                  (SPECIAL EVENT HIGHLIGHTING
                   OPENING OF NEW CELLAR)

                  ------------------------------------------------

                  JANE IS AVAILABLE FOR MEDIA INTERVIEWS OCTOBER
                  18 and the MORNING OF OCTOBER 19.

                  ------------------------------------------------

WHERE:            At your studio/office or at Davison's

SUGGESTED         .   Chili Madness--
TOPICS OF             (origins, lore and foolproof preparation
DISCUSSION:          tips)
                  .   Chili Tasting
                  .   Inside secrets of Santa Fe/Tex-Mex cooking

                              I I I
```

The concise fact sheet should have title, name, address & telephone number at the top of the page.

example: Michael Riva is the production designer for the Neil Simon movie "Slugger's Wife." He grew up in the theatre. His dad is an art director, his mom an actress, and his grandmother is Marlene Dietrich.

Include very brief background: birthplace, college, etc. It may strike rapport with the producer or the TV host, and every little connection helps.

The Media Kit

The Fact Sheet

This single page lists the event, spokesperson, date of the promotional materials and the address. It is clearly a "quick-look" page designed to give the producer ready-reference information.

Background Information

These pages cover basic statistics, facts and current updates on the subject to be covered. Producers need up-to-the-minute background material that enhances the newsworthiness of the segment. These pages should be only 1 or 2 pages in length, double spaced. Information to be included:
- Why is this subject worth covering?
- How can it benefit viewers?
- How many people does it affect?
- What are the costs?
- Are there related events of interest to viewers? If so, give times and dates of seminars, workshops.

Suggested Questions

Some media kits contain a list of questions that might be helpful to the producer. They indicate key points to be covered and suggest a variety of approaches to the subject. They can also create a sense of curiosity if they are imaginative.

For example, "Why would a veterinarian want to leave a comfortable practice to establish a cookie company?"

Staff Photos by Art Hager

By Jim Landberg
Staff Writer

S he's been credited with originating the American country look in decorating. She's been called the first lady of American country decor and refers to herself as "Miss Country."

She is Mary Ellison Emmerling, a city woman whose blending of the contemporary and the primitive became her trademark during a six-year stint on the decorating pages of Mademoiselle magazine.

Emmerling says she had no idea at the outset that she was creating a particular style. The New York City woman had decorated her apartment with items she liked: folk art, quilts, pillows and antiques that contrasted with her white walls and her white contemporary sofas. When the place attracted the New York Times and House and Garden, Emmerling knew she was onto something.

Soon she became decorating editor at House Beautiful, and her first book, "American Country," was published in 1980.

Now she has a second book, "Collecting American Country" (Clarkson N. Potter, Inc., 276 pages, $35), which has been out about six weeks.

Emmerling autographed books at the south Minneapolis antique shop.

"Country pieces are being used more and more in the homes and apartments of today," she said during a recent visit to Minneapolis. "Even the most modern of homes are often being decorated with country items." Emmerling said that in her books she tries to instill confidence in people to use country items in their decorating.

That point is well-illustrated in her latest work. It has about 400 photos, most of them in color, showing single items, collections and rooms decorated in variations on the country theme.

For openers, "Collecting American Country" is an alphabet soup of collectibles from A to Z (advertising tins to Zanesville, Ohio, sewer-pipe animals). In between are cookie cutters, embroidery, hearts, ironstone, molds, owls, rocking horses, Santas, squeak toys, Valentines, whimsies, weather vanes, whirligigs and more. A color photo, brief history and description of each are included in the first chapter.

Emmerling devotes one chapter to the folk artists of today. Here are potters,

weavers, furniture builders and other artisans applying 18th- and 19th-century techniques. "Most people today don't care if an item is old or new," she said "Today, what is important is if an item is well-made.

"They want the country look, but they want quality, too. . . . I think things like the wooden toys made today are the antiques for our children and grandchildren."

Advice on how to care for country treasures makes up a third chapter. Here Emmerling shares preservation tips she has gleaned from the experts. Want to clean a teddy bear? This chapter tells how and also gives responses to questions oft-asked of the author in her lectures and visits to antique shops around the country.

Is your tinware taking over? Are those bushels of baskets a bother? Tired of ducking your decoys? Relax. "Ways to Display" and "Living with Collections" are chapters that emphasize integrating country pieces into the home.

This clipping from the
Minneapolis Tribune *doubled as*
a biography for the author.

The Media Kit

This is a service to the producer, but don't assume they will be the only questions asked. Guests should be prepared to answer any question on their subject.

Clippings

Enclose a couple of reprints of articles about yourself, your service or your product. It gives the producer confidence that you are newsworthy, and often quotes or insights from the story are used in the interview.

If you don't have any clippings, work on getting newspaper coverage. The print media and electronic media are impressed with each other.

Do not send long, academic pieces. TV is generally a medium to give the layperson information, and the producer, as well as the viewer, is probably a layperson concerning your subject.

Photographs and Visuals

All media kits contain black and white glossies. They are more useful to newspapers than TV. They serve TV only in putting a face with the spokesperson's name. Horizontal color slides are affordable and are better suited for TV. Electronically sophisticated TV stations can make vertical slides work. They can also color black and white pictures, but often there is not time. The easier you make the job, the better you will look.

Do you have videotape that will add visual support to your apearance? Do you have a videotape of yourself as a good TV guest? Offer this in your kit.

Coming Up Next

Visuals enhance every subject. A picture (slide, videotape, demonstration) is worth a thousand words. It can illustrate a subject and add excitement and interest to any TV appearance.

Don't let your media kit leave home or the office

DELL PUBLISHING CO., INC.
1 Dag Hammarskjold Plaza/245 East 47th Street/New York, N.Y. 10017/Telephone (212) 605-3000/Telex 238781 DELL

SUGGESTED QUESTIONS FOR DISCUSSION WITH DR. IRENE C. KASSORLA

1. What is your definition of a winner? A loser? How are they different?

2. Generally, how do winners and losers approach new situations? What is the difference in their attitudes?

3. Are men or women more likely to fall into a winning pattern? A losing pattern? Why?

4. Why are so many people not only afraid of failure, but of success as well?

5. All we've been hearing lately is this slogan of yours, "Give Yourself A Kiss!". Do you mean we should reward ourselves even if we fail?

6. What are some ways to turn a losing streak into a winning one? Is there a surefire formula for winning? Aren't some people just more resourceful, smarter, richer than others? Aren't some people just born winners?

7. How can you compare Malcolm Forbes and Diane von Furstenberg to the average person? Did they have to overcome great obstacles to get where they are or did they start off in a better position? Why should the average man or woman ever hope to attain such awesome levels of success?

8. Can you apply the winner/loser approach to any situation in life? What are some examples?

9. From your list of accomplishments, it's easy to see that you're a winner. How did you become the winner that you are today?

10. What have you not accomplished that you'd like to do in the future? How do you plan to accomplish it?

11. The word is out that you're up at the crack of dawn and always working. What kind of day do you have? Is there a formula you follow to direct the course of your life?

12. You write about "talking your way into success." What do you mean by this?

13. How do people fall into losing patterns? Is it environmental? Biological? How can a child start early on a winning path?

14. You talk about taking chances and mention "The Uncomfortable, Anxiety Road" versus "The Comfortable, No Anxiety Road." Is a winner more open to change than a loser? Why or why not? Which path would a winner take?

15. If you had just a few words of advice to give someone who we would classify as a "loser," what would those words be?

This questionnaire highlights Dr. Kassorla as an expert, not another author plugging a book.

without examples of what viewers could cast their hungry eyes upon.

In the next chapter, we'll talk about how to be picture-perfect like the pros.

Bump—What do chefs, fashion designers and plastic surgeons do best? Create eye-catchers!

Picture This—
The Importance of
Visuals

Botanist Dr. Helen Henke demonstrated plant-care techniques and offered viewers a free plant-care guide.

What's the most effective way to make a TV viewer sit up and take notice? Visuals—eye-catchers, pictures with appeal, or "wiggle" as we refer to videotape.

Television is a visual medium. *Viewers* tune into "Eye-witness News Reports." Videotape footage attracts attention and helps to communicate news information. Sports footage and instant replays put the viewer in the midst of the action and add a new dimension to the sports coverage never known before. Even certified meteorologists have become visual experts. Weather reports are given with lively illustrations of sun and clouds. Actual footage of tornado, flood, ice and snow scenes and the ever-changing weather maps give viewers a visual sense of current weather conditions. Television doesn't just tell you, it shows you!

If meteorologists can come up with effective "show and tell" reports, so can computer experts, financial analysts and authors. Spokespersons today must concern themselves not only with *what* information they give, but *how* they present that information visually. It has been proven that people remember 20 percent of what they have heard and 80 percent of what they have seen and heard.

Viewers who have grown up in the television generation are more accustomed to receiving information and forming opinions from visuals than from the printed word. Videotape, slides, photographs and other visuals transmit ideas, stimulate imagination and produce action. Picture images of a book's cover remain long after the words pertaining to the new book have been reported. Seeing is believing!!!

What Are Visuals?

Free booklets and send-ins reinforce your message and allow you to put information into the hands of potential customers.

Visuals are pictures that illustrate your story and reinforce your message. TV commercials are the best examples of how to tell or sell an idea with pictures. Visuals for television can come from many sources:

- *Videotapes* for television are produced on 2-inch, 1-inch or ¾-inch sizes. One-half-inch Beta or VHS tapes, used in home videocassette machines, are *not* broadcast quality. We were sent ½-inch tapes on several occasions when we requested visual support but were never able to use them because they were below standard for broadcast.

- *Photographs and Slides* make good illustrations for products, art works, scientific projects, underwater activities, time-lapse events or hundreds of other subjects. Slides should be horizontal for use on television. Product shots should include a person using the product rather than the product alone. Magazine pictures are excellent visuals, but they are under copyright laws and should not be used without permission.

- *Demonstrations,* live or on tape, can show how products or services can be used. Make-up sessions, cooking techniques, plumbing tools and camping gear all act as a hook to draw the viewer's attention and communicate quickly what might take a great deal of time to explain.

- *Artwork, Graphics and Posters* are best used as quick references. They add color but lack movement. They can be incorporated with other stills in creating animated visuals on tape (see *How to Acquire and Use Videotape*).

Posters are excellent visuals to use for TV cameras at meetings or demonstrations. Posters that read "We Want Jobs" or "Stop the Greedy Developers" are an effective way of getting your message across on television.

- *Charts and Graphs* have limited use. They are visuals used by doctors or experts in real estate, insurance or investments. They are often too complicated and rarely stay on the screen long enough to give a clear explanation.
- *Available Video* such as news footage, movie clips or industry tapes can be bought and re-edited to provide visual support for television. The cost of editing available footage is far less expensive than the cost of producing it.

   Imagine a brides segment using a movie clip of Elizabeth Taylor in "Father of the Bride" dissolving into news footage of Princess Di's wedding with an added shot of Daisy Mae on her wedding day to show the universality of the bride.
- *Media Events* are events performed because they will look good in the newspapers or on television.

   Six Flags Over Georgia opens one new ride each year. They invite the press to cover the ride in action. It is timely and visual and usually makes the 6:00 p.m. news.

   Politicians stage media events by spending the night in ghettos or shaking workers' hands at factories. The American Cancer Society stages media events where they nail cigarettes into a coffin to dramatize the effects of smoking. *Any*where Prince or Madonna appear is a media event.
- *Send-ins, Information Booklets and Brochures* attract attention and reinforce your message. They also allow you to put information directly into the hands of potential customers and to measure viewer response.

   Weber Grill offers a free recipe booklet to viewers. You can be sure that these recipes cook best on a Weber Grill.

Picture This— The Importance of Visuals

Visual accessories also enhance your message. Aprons, patches, T-shirts catch the viewer's eye.

Cameraman Willis Boyd video-tapes handyman Bill Yanson's how-to demonstrations.

Osmose Wood Products offers a free booklet on do-it-yourself weekend projects when their handyman Bill Yanson appears on TV. Most of those weekend do-it-yourselfers will naturally be working on projects that are made with wood.

Copies of a booklet or brochure should be sent to the producer in advance with the appropriate address or address slide.

If viewers mail their requests directly to you or your company, be sure that you are set up to handle the requests. Irritated viewers who have not received their information in a reasonable length of time turn to the station for satisfaction and the producer gets caught in the middle—a position he/she neither likes nor appreciates. Do your job. Deliver promptly.

- *Visual Accessories, Logos* such as a sash or crown from a beauty contest, a T-shirt from a race, a karate jacket or a team shirt are good communicators of your message. Company logos can be reproduced on a variety of items quite easily.

Brad Sears, the popular host of the PBS series "Last Chance Garage," wears a patch with the logo of his show on his mechanic's shirt when he appears on TV.

Jane Butel, author of six books on southwestern cooking and owner of Pecos Valley Spice Products, dresses to sell. On our show she wore a colorful fringed sweater, red leather pants, boots and a cowboy hat. Her thoroughly western look had tremendous eye appeal and immediately related the viewer to her subject.

The Friends of the Atlanta Public Library held "Smorgasbook," a book sale with "literary tastes that appeal to all appetites." The guest from the library wore an apron with the library's logo and a chef's hat. Both made interesting visuals.

- *A Character Generator* is the machine that electronically superimposes names, titles, scores or other written information on the screen. It can also be used to reinforce your spoken message. Seeing words as well as hearing them adds clarity. If your segment lends itself to this kind of visualization, discuss this idea with your producer.

  "The Phil Donahue Show" often uses this technique on video quizzes. Quiz words are spoken, then reinforced by type (font).

  Walter Cronkite tells about speech-making. As he describes the components of a good presentation, words appear on the screen:

  Analyze audience
  Define purpose
  Prepare
    Open
    Body
      Attention-getters
      Logical patterns
      Support for main points
    Close

  This is an effective TV technique, but it requires careful planning.

- *Symbols and Gestures* are visual shorthand. A heart, cross or golden arches communicate a message without the use of words at all. It may be possible for you to create your own "thumbs-up" type of visual.

  Psychologist Dr. Irene C. Kassorla used an interesting symbol when she gave pointers on how to stay on a diet or reach a goal and not become discouraged. She recommended that you reward yourself for the good diet days or deeds by giving yourself a kiss. Then she held up two fingers, kissed them and patted each cheek with the kiss.

Picture This— The Importance of Visuals

49

"Buddy" and Anne Louise Zachary appeared coast to coast promoting Purina's Great American Dog contest. Children and dogs are a winning TV combination.

This gesture demonstrated how viewers could praise themselves for success rather than punish themselves for failures. It was a memorable, easy-to-recall and effective symbol.

A *New York Times* article on the presidential debate talked about the importance of gestures. "On TV, gestures are full of meaning. TV is a performance medium, and by performance the candidates are judged."

- *Picture Words* create immediate images in the mind of the viewer. Examples are good word pictures. When asked, "What does this machine do?," don't answer, "Oh, it is very effective around the house. It can do many household chores." Answer in specifics. "This rack is useful for hanging up wet bathing suits, men's ties or ladies' necklaces."

Using word pictures or specific examples is especially effective when discussing charitable causes. Get the listener involved in donating money because "he will be part of the solution to help crippled children buy braces, have access to therapists or get training for wheelchair sports."

Demonstrations are an entirely different type of visual presentation. They require careful organization. Demonstrations of recipes, tye-dyeing, make-overs, new products, flower arrangements, gifts or camping gear draw the viewer's attention. They communicate information quickly and vividly and make long explanations unnecessary. They help viewers understand how to use products more efficiently. An effective demonstration requires practice and preparation. Use this checklist to organize your demonstration:

**Picture This—
The Importance
of Visuals**

*Checklist for Effective
Demonstrations*

An early American costume added color and interest to a demonstration of a "down-home" herb recipe.

- Go through the demonstration thoroughly with an associate or professional several times until you are comfortable and look natural with the presentation.
- Make a supply checklist.
- Practice packing, re-packing and clean-up procedures with your supplies.
- Don't assume that the station will have anything more than a table. Check to make sure they have that. You will often have to bring your own grill, oven, microwave or stands for displaying items.
- Call ahead to check on wiring and special plugs if you need them.
- Bring paper towels and plastic bags for clean up. Sometimes you will have to take away the dirty tools of your trade and will need more plastic bags to handle them.
- Chefs from out of town often hire local home economists to buy staples such as fruits, meats and vegetables and bring them to the station. Often they contract with them to prepare the final product, bring the necessary ingredients for the demonstration and assist them at the station.
- Craft, plumbing, or refinishing demonstrations should be simple so that you can talk and demonstrate without anxiety. Don't plan to demonstrate too much. Design the demonstration in a 1-2-3- process. We call this the "dump-dump-do" technique. "Dump" this and "dump" that and "do" this and you'll have the perfect pudding pie (end result).
- While you are doing your demonstration, relate it to the host, viewers or audience. If possible, give the host a job so that he/she can participate.

Greek cook Maria Sharp demonstrated the preparation of terapitas effectively in less than three minutes. In that time viewers learned the meaning of terapitas (cheese triangles) and got a visual description of folding thin filo dough "like you fold the American flag." We commented on her ease with the filo dough and how comfortable she seemed on her first TV appearance. Her response, "I practiced."

*How to Acquire
and Use Videotapes*

Videotape, using live action or animated stills, can be produced at television stations or at commercial video companies. Check the Yellow Pages for the names of these companies or call a local television station and ask if their facilities are available for rent for outside work.

Independent camerapersons, sound engineers and editors at television stations often do free-lance projects. The chief photographers or news assignment editor at the station can give you names and information.

Live Action Videotape can be an exciting way of presenting your bathing suit designs, showcasing your singing group or demonstrating your robot creation. Before you call a cameraperson or video production house, do your homework.

1. *Decide on what you need.*

If you are doing a novel on Border Collies, a 30-second videotape of dogs in action, playing with their master or going through the paces of herding sheep, could enhance your television appearance. Getting sound as well as pictures could require a sound engineer as well as a cameraperson.

If you want complete coverage of a water-skiing competition to use for future promotions as well as television interviews, you may need a full crew with several cameras and sound equipment.

If you are going to sell ½-inch videos on how to order wines for use on home videos, they can be originally produced on ¾-inch tape and then dubbed

James Breedlove creates a video. Some news camerapersons free-lance.

Video News Release

on to ½. This will give the option of having several tapes for sale or for use on broadcast appearances. You cannot, however, record on ½-inch, Beta or VHS tape and then dub it up to ¾-inch tape. It is not broadcast quality.

2. *Determine how much money you have to spend.*

Production costs include cameras, lights, audio equipment, studio facilities, editing, etc. They can range from $500-$3,000 for one minute of ¾-inch videotape. Talent, costumes, musicians, make-up experts, props, etc. are not included in these costs. In-studio production is generally cheaper than production done on location.

Production costs may seem high, but if you compare them to the cost per viewer, they may run as little as pennies per person.

3. *Ask questions of the people you are considering.*
   - Do they have a reel or tape of work that you can see?
   - Can they give references?
   - How long will the work take?
   - Which elements will they provide? What must you provide?
   - How can you cut costs?
   - How much will extra copies (dubs) of the tape cost?

The video news release is the newest step in visual PR. *Public Relations Journal*, October 1985, explains this client-generated news product which is made available to television stations.

One of the latest public relations tools, the "video news release" (VNR), is designed to resemble a news feature, complete with on-the-spot interviews and narration. VNRs are also known as "electronic press releases" (EPRs) and "newsclips." Most range in length from 90 seconds to two minutes.

Video news releases are not commercials, although they often display a specific product. In contrast to a commercial, a VNR is aired on a news show, the most credible time slot on television. Its purpose is to communicate "a controlled client message," says Burson-Marsteller producer Lee Migliara. Because more people watch news shows than any other television segment, VNRs aired on the news or on a news show such as "Good Morning America" have the potential to reach an enormous number of viewers.

Product-related VNRs aim to tie the product name to a newsworth event. This year, when the makers of Arm & Hammer baking soda were working out their public relations program with Burson-Marsteller, it was easy to come up with a news-linked VNR: Arm & Hammer baking soda is being used to clean the Statue of Liberty for its centennial.

VNRs are also used as *the* corporate statement in a news crisis situation, and tape of corporate news conferences also provides material for television.

The video news release is controversial. At this time, television stations use the VNRs, but there is resistance from news directors. It is a new product says the *Public Relations Journal*.

They [news directors and editors] must have felt the same when they first got print press releases. As it becomes familiar, they'll use it the same way: edit it, take the story, or use it the way it is.

Videotapes of varying length can be produced as a news feature to be used in various TV markets. The master tape can be re-edited to use as introductory or interview video for a TV guest appearance.

When ScotTowel Jr. introduced its new 8-inch towel they used 2 videos. The first was a news-style feature that explained the money and manpower necessary to bring a

Picture This— The Importance of Visuals

Making a Video News Release or Support Visuals for a TV Appearance

new product to market. The estimated cost of more than 3 million dollars which went into product development was used as the news hook. The example of a new product was the 8-inch ScotTowel, Jr.

The second tape used on talk shows highlighted kitchen tips by an organizational expert who used the new towel as part of her timesaving tips. A booklet with additional ideas was also offered. This tape was used on talk shows as visual support when the efficiency expert appeared as a guest.

According to A. Brown-Olmstead Associates, the PR firm that handled this client, these tapes were seen in the targeted southeastern region by more than 1,250,000 viewers in 11 major cities.

The proposed visuals for consumer videos or TV guest-appearances support video can include visuals from a variety of sources such as products shots, news footage, movie footage, historical photographs or possible comments from relevant people (man-on-the-street comments). Music that relates to a particular era or event also helps to hook viewers.

Introductory Clip

A 30-second introduction tape can be used at the opening of the segment as the host introduces the guest. It would include background visuals of the guest, a variety of uses for a product, or pictures from a book. A voice-over script could accompany the video.

Interview Video Clip

A 45-second clip of video material can be used during the interview to illustrate the book, product or service involved. The materials used will be different from the 30-second introductory clip.

This clip can be used by television stations in areas where the author or spokesperson does not appear. It offers a 1½-2 minute news or feature length interview clip complete with a written introduction for the host. The clip would include video materials used in clips #1 and #2, a narration by news talent and comments (sound bites) from a variety of involved people.

This is a 4-minute feature or news length interview to be used by cable stations that require longer segments. It would be an extension of clip #2.

Aris Products sent a podiatrist on a TV tour to promote good foot care with a new comfort slipper. They used a very visual clip showing a variety of feet, the different kinds of shoes people wore and how people used their feet, including a funny scene of a baseball player and an umpire who used their feet to "cuss." They also had women-on-the-street answers to the question, "Do your feet hurt?" In less than 30 seconds, every viewer was aware of his feet and ready for information relating to them.

Celebrated photographer Francesco Scavullo knew he would tour for his book. Because he understands TV's love of visuals, he set up a video camera in his studio to record the creative process involved in photographing celebrities such as Brooke Shields, Luciano Pavarotti or Frank Sinatra. He edited the piece, and viewers had a quick look at the master in action when he made his TV tour.

Picture This—
The Importance
of Visuals

*Consumer Information
Clip #1*

Clip #2

Even the fabulous Christy Brinkley was a better guest with fashion tape. We could see her new designs, not just talk about them.

Thirty seconds of videotape can add interest to any television segment. As many as 20 still pictures can be shown easily and interestingly in this space of time. Slides, still photographs or close-up shots taken with a studio camera can be made to twirl, spin, multiply or enlarge by the use of electronic video effects. *Time* magazine often uses this technique in producing its commercials.

This technique can be achieved with the electronic switcher used by television stations or production studios. Because of its simplicity, it is far less expensive than other types of moving visuals. When set to music, these stills can make a dynamic video piece.

The visuals are planned, the media kit is complete. Where do you send it? How do you make contacts? Whom do you call out of town?

Stay tuned. Next we'll tell you how to target your mail and find the right person for your pitch.

How to Develop Contacts

Talk shows focus on personality journalism. Anchor Andrea Nissen and NBC reporter Norma Quarles share career and parenting experiences with viewers.

If it's not what you know but "who" you know, how do you get to know them?

Television's constant and unrelenting need for news and features may make your effort to get to the news assignment editors, talk-show producers or public affairs directors at your local station or even on a national program easier than you might think. With hours of programming to get on the air each week, these people are constantly aware that your call could fill a need.

In an article in *Fortune*, October 14, 1985, Louis Banks, the magazine's former managing editor and now a teacher of business and the media at MIT, described the rewards of becoming a source of information for the media:

> *Perhaps the biggest challenge in the relationship between business and the media in the past three or four years has been this shift in the supply-demand equation of business news. Today the demand is heavy and increasing, making the supply more precious in the marketplace. Companies with sophisticated public relations counsel at their call, can increasingly influence coverage of their businesses over the long term.*

Banks calls it "source power":

> *On the one hand, business and economic reporting has become very professional, and the market is rewarding those who produce that stream of relevant, interesting, and colorful information that makes the system run. On the other hand, many dynamic businesses are willing to take part of the responsibility for the competence they have long demanded in the media. And they find themselves, happily, as almost equal players in the game.*
>
> *In a sense business and the media keep each other honest, for source power is effective over the long run only if it is honest in what it provides. And the information-hungry business press is successful only as long as it has new facts, new ideas, and new learning to pass along to its customers.*

At 11-Alive in Atlanta, health reporter Andrea Nissen and producer Becky Peterzell meet regularly with different hospital personnel and doctors. The resulting relationship is beneficial to both parties. The news is seeking the latest in health information, the health industries want exposure, and when a health crisis arises, each party has a contact.

*What Are the Jobs
of the Principal Contacts and
How Do They Make
Their Decisions?*

News Assignment Editor

A news assignment editor is the pivotal point in a news operation. He handles the news crews, story assignments, in-coming calls, mail and media kits and works with the news director, executive producer and producers to determine the line-up of stories for the major newscasts.

The process of assembling the evening newscast begins at a morning meeting with the news director and producers. They go over a list of possible story ideas. Breaking news stories, satellite feeds and videotape highlights of live telecasts taken from earlier network shows, and a file list of media releases and announcements are discussed. The assignment editor then checks a rundown of news crews, replaces sick or vacationing reporters and photographers and assigns stories, indicating approximate story lengths for each. Radio and phone calls come in constantly—news information, requests for television coverage, news inquiries, viewers' questions and complaints. Story idea calls are relentless.

A giant board is filled in with a list of stories for possible inclusion in the broadcast. Later in the day, the honing process begins. Reporters return to write and edit stories. News story priorities are established. Stories are juggled and arranged according to their importance and the time necessary to cover each event. Decisions are based on timeliness, visual impact, ties to national and world news and stories that illustrate "how people cope."

It is at this point that some stories make or fail "the cut." If it is a slow day, your story may make it. If the day is heavy with news, it may not.

The rundown is completed and typed, and copies are given to the director, technical crew and tape editors. Anchors are given their lead-ins, scripts are completed and, with a final rush of manpower and adrenalin, the news is on the air. This process, in different degrees of intensity, is repeated 4 to 5 times every day.

Talk shows focus on "personality journalism." Hosts talk with people who make events happen or who have had interesting things happen to them. These people are activists and doers from every walk of life, the people who create new products or services that affect the way we live. They are knowns and unknowns who offer stimulating information on sports, finance, music, personal relations, entertainment, health or fitness. They are superstars and they are ordinary people who have been part of extraordinary events. They are people who have a product, service or expertise that will enhance the life of the viewer.

Producers for talk shows are in charge of the overall production of each show. They oversee sets, formats, rundowns, talent, scripts, guests and a dozen other details, including handling in-coming calls and mail and screening media kits. They determine the guests and the line-up of each show. Depending on the size of the staff, they may do all of the above.

The producer may be the on-camera host of the show or the behind-the-scenes coordinator. Unlike news, much of his work, such as scheduling, taping, line-ups and the production of visuals, is done in advance. National talk shows provide make-up artists, dressing areas, meals or refreshments. Local programs rarely have any of these luxuries.

How to Develop Contacts

Talk Show Producers

*Jane Pauley handles 4-to
6-minute interviews or demonstrations with a variety of
interesting guests.*

Talk-show producers are human. They have personal biases and preferences. One may be much more interested in a new dental service or charitable event than another. They are looking for timely, unique and visually interesting personalities to make their shows important to their viewers. It is your job to customize your information, to create excitement and interest in your product, cause or service, which will fulfill the needs of their programs.

Talk show programs fall into four main categories:

- *News and Feature Magazine Programs* offer a combination of news and feature segments. "The Today Show," "Good Morning America" and "Morning News" are good examples of this kind of format. News and feature producers work side by side to fill the time segments for which they are responsible.

  Interview segments for news or feature guests are generally very short, between 4-6 minutes. They include guests such as economists, politicians, stars, heroes, ordinary people with unusual stories, or new-product creators. They also feature guests who do demonstrations for crafts, cooking, exercise, etc. Programs using this kind of format are produced on both national and local levels.

- *Personality Interviews and Demonstration Programs* have strictly feature-oriented formats and do not include any news segments. These programs are designed around a single host such as Gary Collins of "Hour Magazine," Merv Griffin or Johnny Carson.

  Guests for morning, afternoon or late-night talk shows differ. Daytime guests tend to be celebrities or people who do more how-to cooking or fitness demonstrations. Some are chosen because they offer a personal insight into what it's like to be an Olympic competitor, a lottery winner, a rock star or a teenage hero.

  Late-night guests are more entertainment oriented.

All guests, however, must be the kind of people viewers want to visit with in their kitchens, den, office or bedrooms.

- *Single Issue Talk Shows* like the "Phil Donahue Show" or "Woman To Woman" focus the entire format of the program on one subject such as single parenting or the changing role of men. Sunday news conferences or public affairs programs often use this format. Subjects are chosen from national or local topics of interest.

  Subjects for in-depth discussion shows often come from ideas presented in media kits. The subject of these programs is always timely. Once the subject is decided upon, it is the job of a producer to find supporting guests or experts to talk about it from a variety of viewpoints.

- *Evening Magazine Shows* like "Entertainment Tonight," "P.M. Magazine" or the "Barbara Walters Specials" are feature-oriented programs. They use taped interviews of interesting people such as nationally-known puppeteer Jim Henson or a local hot air balloon-maker. These interviews are shot on location and offer visual insights as well as comments from personalities.

  The "P.M." programs were designed to give national distribution and publicity to programs with local appeal. Local hosts introduce taped segments produced by their station or sent to them from other "P.M." stations. The "best" of the "P.M." segments get air play in many different cities.

The public affairs director is the link between the station and the community. The public owns the airwaves. The broadcast industry, in exchange for the right to license these air rights, has a responsibility to promote the community and its needs on the air.

How to Develop Contacts

Willard Scott promotes good causes based on clever attention-getting props.

Public Affairs Director

Camerapersons, reporters, sales staff and management are possible contacts.

Public affairs directors have three primary areas of responsibility: to work on projects that link the station with the community, to create on-air public affairs programs and to produce public service announcements (PSAs).

Their work with the community includes scheduling station tours with groups, coordinating fund-raising events with a variety of non-profit organizations, sponsoring Community Can-A-Thons or Feed the Hungry Drives, or scheduling station stars and workers for local appearances or major TV events such as the Jerry Lewis telethons. They represent the station in community discussions with local leaders on such social issues as child abuse or education.

They work with community organizations and citizens to create interview programs on cultural activities, health-related programs, senior citizens' problems, children's programming or social issues. They coordinate and produce on-air commentaries by people in the community who want to speak on issues.

The public is constantly in contact with the public affairs director, particularly when they want to get free television exposure for a non-profit event. One of the most effective ways to get your message on the air is to write to the PA director several weeks in advance requesting a public service announcement. Those people who give plenty of notice are in the minority and stand a much better chance of getting a message on air.

Send a letter with all of the necessary information and then be sure to follow up with a call. Public affairs directors work very hard to meet the needs of the communities, but they also appreciate people who prepare their message with timeliness, uniqueness or visual interest.

Promote your cause on the air by thinking in terms of tie-ins with current issues. If you know a station is airing a dramatic story about a child who has been abused, contact them about airing a PSA on a clinic that provides support to families suffering with this problem.

If you are coordinating a benefit, think in terms of uniqueness. A salute to unsung community heroes not only might offer the public affairs department a hook, but might also generate an interest in the news department by providing a good local human-interest story.

Many companies have discovered one simple secret of free on-air recognition: they support community events. Donations of company volunteers for telethons, of building materials for staging events, of company trucks for collections, or of company soft drinks for events benefiting the community help to get their names before the public. Companies' names are associated with the support of a worthwhile community cause and at the same time are given free on-air recognition.

How to Develop Contacts

How to Make Local Contacts

If you live near the station you're trying to contact, it is mandatory that you do your homework and watch the programming. You can learn the names of reporters and the formats of the shows that might be appropriate for your information. The best way to get the names of the people behind the scenes is to talk to the switchboard operator. Ask her who books guests, makes news decisions or handles public affairs. Be dogged about finding out who the decision-makers are. Don't waste time on others. Get the correct spelling and pronunciation of their names.

News assignment editors usually answer incoming calls at the news desk and take the information. Getting to a news director is more difficult. Stick with the assignment editor. When talking to a news assignment editor, talk-show producer or public affairs director, it is important to have your information at your fingertips. The continually changing aspect of this business allows him or her only a brief time to hear you out. Your information is best presented as a follow-up to the media kit you have already sent.

Reporters are often good contacts. If a reporter has done a story related to an idea you have, call and compliment him/her on the approach or depth of the report. Discuss your idea with him. Ask his advice or offer to work with him. Build a relationship.

Camerapersons can also be good contacts. They are behind-the-scenes people who rarely get attention from the public. If you see a story well done visually, ask the news assignment editor who shot it and call to express your appreciation. Although he/she isn't involved in the decision-making process, he could help to direct you to the decision-maker.

Personal Contacts Count

If you have access to any television personnel—use it! The personal approach in any business is always important. Repay the favor by offering a well thought-out idea.

The sales staff is a good avenue into the station. If you advertise, ask your sales rep about developing a demonstration or how-to segment about your product or service for a talk show or offer a news segment on how new laws or current trends in your industry affect consumers.

If you don't advertise but have a friend who does, ask him/her to speak to his sales rep for you. A good rep is always interested in helping his clients. Keep the rep involved in the process until the right media contact is made and you can take over. Don't let him just turn you over to a "name."

Television personnel from the general manager to the custodial employees do volunteer work. The agencies and organizations for which they work have a personal and important appeal for them. Their knowledge of events or activities can stimulate the public affairs director or talk-show producers to create a good public service announcement or interview segment for television. If you are in a non-profit organization, always ask your volunteers what television contacts they have.

Television stations must be responsive to the needs of the community. The public owns the airwaves, and it is the job of the Federal Communications Commission (FCC) to license the airwaves to stations that will address these needs. Stations that fail to meet these commitments could lose their license to operate. These laws are changing, but most stations will continue to have a strong commitment to their community.

It is also important to realize that in the non-profit world, "doing good" is not "doing enough." You must also do your homework to gain media support. Competition for free air time is just as keen in this area as in all other areas of television. You must create an attractive event or plan an informative news or public affairs program or a PSA to catch their attention.

You must give them written information about the event, including the "who," "what," "where" and "why" facts. Information about relevant visuals should also be included. Some television stations have a policy about the events they promote. Call well in advance for information concerning the event you wish to promote. The public affairs department is one of the most understaffed areas of television. They can't create or plan ideas for you, but they can help you get your well-designed plans on the air.

Television likes experts. The definition of an "expert" is "anyone who lives more than 50 miles from home." Sometimes it is easier to sell yourself to media in other cities than to your own hometown station.

There are books available in the public libraries with listings of the names, addresses and phone numbers of

How to Develop Contacts

The telephone is the heartline of the talk show. Producer Tracy Green develops a segment with a future guest.

Making Contacts Out-of-Town— Qualifying Calls

Producer Ellen Berman must fill specific segments of the show. Know the format before you request an appearance.

If at First
You Don't Make Contact,
Call, Call Again!

all the television stations. Having good information on stations or shows increases your chances of making a sale.

Call out-of-town stations and ask the switchboard for the same information used in making local contacts. Call the appropriate contact and check to see if this is a good time to ask a few questions. Ask about the program formats, the kinds of segments he/she is interested in, the kinds of segments he is not interested in. Ask when is the best time to contact him to schedule segments, what are his scheduling deadlines and lengths of segments, whether he has live or taped interviews. Confirm the name, title and address of the proper contact.

This is a "query" call, not a "sale" call, and most media people will give you this information willingly. Unlike annoying calls made by salespeople to solicit business, media personnel expect these calls and respect people who do their homework before making a pitch. These kinds of calls save you time. You don't want to make your pitch to the wrong person.

Media people are very hard to reach because the news is always changing and they need to move quickly to make their deadlines. Don't be discouraged if it takes 6, 12, or 20 calls before you make contact. As they said in "The Godfather," "it's not personal, it's just business." Television stations are usually short-staffed. In addition to handling all of their own typing, phones and incoming mail, producers also must work with editors, the art department and the production staff to get the show on the air on schedule.

Take heart. When a contact is hard to reach, most people give up. But you can't make a sale until you reach the decision-maker. Fighting the frustration will pay off.

You might be surprised at the number of people who

send press releases, letters, even expensive media kits and never call or call only a few times and give up. It's trite but true, "the squeaky wheel does get the oil"—and the attention. The media kit without persistent follow-up never makes it off the stack or on the air.

When you finally do make contact, it can be the beginning of a relationship that will make you a valuable television resource. When a change in the IRA regulations made news, the assignment editor remembered a well-versed and articulate "Noonday" guest and interviewed her on the subject for the 6:00 p.m. news. They have stayed in touch, and the financial expert has become a resource for the assignment editor.

Returning calls can be a problem in the media. If you leave a message concerning information on a recent murder, a life-threatening event or a top celebrity, you will usually get a return call immediately.

If your message is not that urgent but interesting, such as a good tip on a local record-breaker, a unique product break-through or ideas for an upcoming holiday, you get a call back.

Pique an interest, create curiosity when you want a call returned. Then be sure there is someone with a pencil or an answering machine to take the call if you are away. If you don't get the call, don't be discouraged. Call, call, call again.

One last note on media calls. If you call someone in media to whom you have previously spoken, don't start out with "Hi, this is Ann." State your name and the subject you've been talking about before you leap into a conversation. When you hear the "click" of recognition, then start to talk. Repeat your name and subject again at the end of the call.

How to Develop Contacts

Returning Phone Calls

"Hi, This Is Ann"

The "Noonday" pediatrician
Sandy Matthews, author of
Through The Motherhood Maze,
was "discovered" at a cocktail
party.

Media people get calls from 30-50 sources a day. They *need* and *appreciate* your opening reminder.

It is a lot of work, making contacts, thinking up story ideas with a news hook, making a PSA. Why bother? Whether you are promoting a product or a civic event, your promotion effort on television is your *outside salesman.* When the volunteer goes to sell tickets or to ask for money, if the prospect has seen something about the subject on television, that person has an immediate frame of reference. "Oh yes, I saw something about that on television..." Your "outside salesman" has opened the door.

If Coke, Pepsi and Panasonic can sell their idea or product to you in a commercial that only takes 30 to 60 seconds, then you need to be prepared to make your pitch and sell your idea to television just as quickly.

You're the expert. *You* have enthusiasm. *You* know your idea or product. It's what's up front that counts when you're trying to make your sell to the media.

Next... "How to Pitch Like a Pro"

How to Develop Contacts

Is It Worth the Effort?

Coming Up Next

75

How to Pitch Like
a Pro

A national news story in USA Today *or* Time *is a good hook for a local story on the same subject.*

How do you make a TV producer an offer of a guest he/she can't afford to refuse?

When the pros make their pitch to the media, they begin with a good media kit and the names of the right contacts. They also have the basic elements of good salesmanship: a winning attitude, a strong self-image, brevity and flexibility. Cultivating these elements also can be a great fear-fighter for those who are not-so-pro.

The pros also know that timing is important, and before they begin their conversation on the telephone with the contact, they ask if it is a good time to talk. If it is, they go for it.

Enthusiasm is contagious—so is the lack of it. Producers appreciate enthusiasm and want to be convinced that you are offering them a good media story. They want to feel that you are knowledgeable and that you understand their needs and those of their viewers. Think of yourself as a problem-solver, an expert. Don't be timid. "Psych" yourself to win!

Good telephone openers begin with your name, an inquiry as to whether the person has received your media kit and then a comment such as:

- "I have a unique (fashion, medical) segment I think you might be interested in."

Follow that by mentioning a contact's name if you have one. Other openers begin:

- "I specialize in the (diet, beauty) field and there is an important new (product, service) that I think might help your viewers to _____."
- "Perhaps you've seen the recent article in *Newsweek* and *USA Today* on _____. I think you might be interested in following up this national story with a local story on _____."

How to Pitch Like a Pro

Good Openers

- "The movie 'The Karate Kid' is having a big impact on young people in our city. All the karate schools have experienced a giant boom in enrollment, and I thought you might be interested in a segment on what some 'real' karate kids that I teach are doing."

It's what's up front that counts, so open with the most important facts: a new breakthrough (a revolutionary new toothpaste), the youngest or oldest achiever (a 16-year-old acting student who just signed on an ABC soap opera), an outstanding statistic (82,000 Bibles sold daily), an interesting background (Ruth Handler, creator of the Ken and Barbie dolls, is now developing breast prosthesis since her mastectomy), a new consumer service (consumers can change the color of their eyes with new soft-color contact lenses in different colors), a "first" (home robot for under $50), an interesting character (Famous Amos, the author of the book *The Face That Launched a Thousand Chips*). If your organization is recognized in some particular way (raised $100,000 for retarded citizens last year), mention it.

Read magazine travel ads or house-for-sale ads to learn how to put your most important and eye-catching information up front with a minimum of words. These ads have a limited amount of space to pique your interest and give their main points. You can't sell 'em if you don't tell 'em what's important and why—*immediately*!

How to Handle Objections

Don't be put off by a lack of interest or "We don't usually use this kind of story." An objection is not a rejection. It means the person wants to know more. Be flexible. Help them to say, "Yes." Approach the idea with slightly different facts and information. Tell them who else is interested, how many people will be affected, what visuals you have to offer and why this is newsworthy.

One coffee company representative called at least 6 times before she finally made contact. There wasn't any interest in a coffee segment unless it had a "hook" or some new, fresh approach. The caller continued to be pleasant, offering different alternatives. Finally, she said, "It's a new way of entertaining, especially at holiday time."

A segment on how to entertain with coffee instead of cocktails followed. The quick and easy coffee demonstration was not only new, it was a good tie-in to current legislation on DUI laws.

Another caller offered a segment on travel information. We had a daily feature on travel and weren't really interested in more. Undeterred, she started talking about a new machine for learning how to water-ski on land. That *was* new! If she could put together slides or tape on the machine, we could work something out. The conversation took less than 5 minutes. She had her information at her fingertips and could switch approaches quickly and effectively.

It may help to create a sense of urgency when faced with objections to mention a local seminar, a performing date or an autographing appearance.

Television people are in the business of presenting current events and understand the importance of being "first" to get information to the viewers. You'd be surprised how media people can move things around when they get interested in an idea. There is a constant reshuffling of the schedule in an effort to be current. When times are slow, your "sell" will be easier. When times are fast, you'd better be hot!

When dealing with objections, ask the producer what it would take to persuade him/her to use your idea. *Listen!* It's a great way to learn. It gives you an opportunity to overcome objections and helps you discover what does appeal. Each station and producer are different and have

How to Pitch Like a Pro

Famous Amos got fresh TV exposure for his cookies with his book, The Face That Launched a Thousand Chips.

Print ads are short and attention-getting. They are good examples of how to pique a producer's interest and make your points quickly.

different needs and requirements. Be prepared to customize your standard information. Don't give up without a polite fight.

Objections are standard operating procedure in television. You are being tested. The media person wants to know if you are a good source, savvy and dependable. They want to be convinced you are knowledgeable enough to judge a good story, guest or segment. They also want to be convinced you have good follow-through and will deliver all elements (visuals, bio, information) on time. As one producer said, "I like to talk to a pro. They make me look like a pro when the segement is terrific."

Remember, it is to the producer's advantage to listen to you. The media and the public are mutually dependent on each other for information. Every good idea that comes in by phone is one less a producer has to go out and dig for.

If you've been successful booking a guest spot or interview, complete your follow-through. Good follow-through means doing what you said you would do—and more. It establishes credibility and reliability.

Be sure to confirm the time, date, address and name of contact. Ask about additional information needed such as length of segment, whether it's a live or taped interview, the name of host or reporter and arrival instructions. ("Ask for Bill at the studio door.") Discuss pictures, props, visuals. If a demonstration is involved, ask about facilities, table, plugs, extension cords. Don't ask what to wear. Sound like a pro and read on. We'll tell you.

If you would like a taped copy of the segment, arrange to have a friend videotape it for you or ask the station how much they charge for this service. Fees vary. Some stations charge one price if you bring your own ¾-inch tape and another if they make the dub and provide the

How to Pitch Like a Pro

*Follow-Up—
The Sign of a Pro*

tape. In some stations the fees may be as high as $100 for this service.

Make good notes at the end of the call. The mind seems to leave us just when we need it most, and although you think you'll never forget the details, you will. Notes are also a good source of protection if you should need it. It is important to be able to document the fact that "you sent a tape on 3/4/85."

Build a Relationship

One or two days before the segment, call and re-confirm the interview. Ask the contact if there are any questions or any additional information he/she might need. Offering "assistance" rather than "asking for something" is a good way to build a relationship for the future. Your call will remind and reassure your contact that you are on the job.

Changes or Cancellations

If it is necessary to communicate bad news, do so as soon as possible. If the guest is sick or if there is a change in the story or information, don't procrastinate—minutes count! Producers have nightmares and wake up shouting, "Where's the guest?"

The producer is going to be upset and changes will need to be made quickly. Generally, if your idea or segment is exciting, he/she will want to reschedule. If not, don't worry unduly that the station will never use you again. The business is so fast-paced they probably won't remember your name if you call to book another idea later. Media people, however, rarely forget the name of someone who doesn't show up for an interview! (Do you hear this, Tova Borgnine!?!)

Still Ahead

Lights, camera, action!!! You've been successful in

getting scheduled. Now it's time to get ready for your media moment. What do you wear, how do you relax, what do you say?

Take a tip from the Boy Scouts and "be prepared."
Next we'll show you how to make your media moment memorable. Stay tuned!

Your Media Moment

Dancer Tommy Tune and actress Betty Thomas meet while waiting to go on "Noonday." Take advantage of the "waiting" time in TV. Meet others, ask questions, work on a project.

What's the secret of becoming a "user-friendly" TV guest?

You're going to be on television. You did a good job in selling your idea. Don't stop now! It is important to plan your personal presentation as well as you planned your media kit presentation. Here is an example of how one young woman failed to go the distance.

She made an initial contact call, sent her material and was diligent about calling again and again. National Hearing Aid month was coming up, and she wanted to promote the in-home, hearing aid testing service her company offered to clients who couldn't or wouldn't go to a doctor or clinic. She had also made the segment newsworthy by tying it to President Reagan's use of a hearing aid and giving statistics on the large number of hearing impaired people in America.

We didn't use the segment that month but later decided to schedule her because we remembered her idea, the service her company offered, and the points she made about people's reluctance to admit their need. On the phone she had been sincere, knowledgeable, seemingly enthusiastic.

Her time came; she panicked. She was informed, but unenthusiastic, boring, and unprepared for TV. She did not help herself, her product or our program. She only went halfway. She prepared *what* she was going to say, but she didn't prepare *how* she was going to say it.

Prepare your mind.

The media kit helped you get your subject in hand. The cover letter focused on how you could entertain and inform viewers. You're an expert—but you can't "wing it."

Helen Gurley Brown, editor of *Cosmopolitan* magazine, appears regularly on the "Tonight Show." "Getting ready is a pleasurable ritual. . . first thinking

Your Media Moment

Ronald Reagan's hearing aid was the perfect news hook for a woman who had an at-home hearing aid service.

*Don't Panic—
Prepare Like a Pro*

through what you're going to say. NO, you don't wing it! Then getting your hair and make-up done to make you look the best you can possibly look—they care. A kiss hello from the show's producer, a wait in the green room and then you're out there acting as though you weren't concerned about whether you're going to be funny.''

Remember:

1. The pros are pros because they prepare.
2. Being known as an entertaining as well as informed guest is the best way of getting asked to be a guest again.

Give the Audience a Gift

When the lights are on and the tape starts to roll, your mind should be in gear. Know the points you want to get across to the viewer so well that they are as automatic as breathing. Whatever the subject, set your mind on the 3 points you want to make and the examples that illustrate these points. Then you will be able to expand or contract these points to fill 3 minutes or 30. These points are the gifts that will enlighten and entertain the viewer.

Three Points from the
Strawberry Fields

One guest offered information on a pick-your-own-strawberry farm. The guest was introduced while tape rolled showing people picking strawberries. The 3 points made by the guest were

1. when and where to pick strawberries (the next 4 weeks will be strawberry-picking season at the farm and the public is invited.)
2. how to pick strawberries and how to tell which are ripe

3. why do it? (It is a fun and economical way to enjoy seasonal fruit.)

*Three Points
from Juice Newton,
Pop Singing Star*

Juice Newton appeared as the spokesperson for the Kidney Foundation. Stars often give their time to worthy causes because they know their celebrity status will help the cause and they want to give something back to people who have made them famous. This kind of promotion also keeps their career in the public eye. She was prepared to give 3 key points:

1. a description of the event she was promoting
2. facts about the disease and how the funds raised would be spent
3. news of her career.

Choosing The Message

Plan a "twinkle" to use in your interview. A "twinkle" is a comment, anecdote, example or fact that is upbeat and ear-catching. Famous chef Julia Child once astounded viewers by confessing her favorite dessert was vanilla ice cream with chocolate sauce. A "twinkle" will help to personalize your message, give you confidence and make your interview memorable.

Don't expect the audience or the host to know anything about your topic (issue, subject). It is your job to explain and define your subject with simple, ordinary, five-cent words. Do not use $15 dollar words or the jargon of your industry unless you can explain it easily (SAG, the Screen Actors Guild). You are trying to enlighten the audience, not impress them. Explain with examples or statistics. (See *Picture Word* in Visuals Chapter.)

Be brief and concise. Give short answers and examples, so the host can move along to the next question, but never give just a "yes" or "no." Monologues are boring and turn off an audience.

In a newspaper interview it is easy to go on and on because the writer will edit your words to fill his space. In a TV interview you must make your 3 points in about 4 minutes. With 30 seconds of introduction and 30 seconds of close, plus the host's questions and the visuals, you will have only about 1 minute per point.

The Practice Interview

Don't leave your TV experience to chance. You are an expert on your subject, but not an expert on TV interviews. *Practice.* Get used to the sound of your own voice answering questions. Get used to answering questions concisely and with good examples. Enlist the help of a friend or a tape recorder.

Make up a list of questions. Give them to a friend or associate. Have the friend interview you using these or any other questions that come to mind. Record it on a tape recorder if possible. Listen to the playback. Did you ramble? Did you make your points? Did you "eh" and "er" and say "like, you know?" How were your examples? Were you an enthusiastic salesperson for your cause? Be critical. Do it again.

If you have video equipment, use it to practice. Don't worry about your looks because the lighting at a TV studio will be better. Do notice your mannerisms and posture. Gestures animate a segment and make you seem more relaxed and in control. Put your hands in your lap with the palms slightly upturned. This will help you remember to use them. Gestures are a natural way to show enthusiasm or emphasize a point. They also help you to relax.

Lean forward. It will give you a sense of interest and energy. Look at the host.

Practice in front of a mirror if you don't have video equipment. Watch yourself in action. Are you animated? Is your expression pleasant? Are your gestures lively? Do you look like you are having a conversation with a friend? Are you relaxed or too intense? Practice until you feel comfortable and natural.

Go to a Pro

There are professional coaches for TV talk shows in large cities. They are often used by corporate spokespersons to help them project a positive image or formulate basic answers to key questions. This service is expensive. It can range from $250 for a group workshop to as much as $2500 for a 6-hour private consultation with a public-speaking expert. Investigate the service and prices in your area. Look under "Speech Instruction" or "Public Speaking" in the Yellow Pages.

The Visual You

What to Wear

The project is to sell your service or product and to package it as well as possible. On TV you are part of the package. Be yourself. Be consistent with the image you wish to convey but not so startling that you distract from the message.

In one city a group worked to have *Playboy-*type magazines removed from the newsstand because they felt the magazines infringed on women's rights. They chose as their spokesperson a messy, unkempt woman who appeared in coveralls. Her appearance was so startling that viewers stared at her instead of listening to her.

Cosmetic company chief Adrian Arpel gives do-it-yourself beauty tips to viewers. Her name and expertise sell her products.

Make-up

She blew it! She had national exposure, but her appearance detracted from her message. Had they chosen an articulate, well-groomed woman, the message would have had impact. Gloria Steinem is certainly a good role model. Women like her as their spokesperson. She has style and substance. Clothes can add or detract from the message you are trying to convey. Decide if you want to telegraph a professional, casual or stylish image.

Patterns, unless you are a fashion pro, can be overpowering. Red gives energy. Red ties on men look particularly good on camera. Black is harsh. Bright blue and bold pink are safe. White is "iffy." It is a hard color for the cameras, but designer Liz Claiborne always wears white and looks terrific. Wear your most becoming color, one that gives you a lift and makes you feel "up."

Watch a talk show or the evening news to see what kind of clothes TV "regulars" and guests wear.

Get expert advice so you will look your best. Most local stations do not have a make-up person, but make-up artists in beauty salons or department stores can give you pointers or make you up for TV.

If you don't like to wear make-up, be yourself, but do use extra blush and color. Don't be too shy to "blush" or you'll blow having an up-beat, on-camera look. Studio lights are bright and will give you a washed out appearance if your make-up is very light. Color gives energy, so don't be afraid to use it for TV.

Men usually don't think about make-up, but there is make-up available to smooth the complexion and tone down the beard. Max Factor makes a product called #8N that is popular with news anchormen, or use a bronze gel for extra color. For shine, use powder or pat your nose and forehead carefully with a handkerchief before going on.

Be Prompt

11:45 a.m. means 11:45 a.m. If you come at 11:30, the producer who has last-minute details to attend to is often hard-pressed to deal with you. If you are early, sit in the lobby and announce your arrival at 11:45 a.m.

TV is a "hurry up and wait" business. You are asked to arrive at a certain time and then you wait. The producer has many variables to deal with at the last minute such as talent, lighting, sound checks, scripts, spelling on supers and preparation of the host. They need to have the assurance that you are there and ready.

In the case of our live noontime show, all guests must arrive at 11:45 a.m. Everyone, from Charlton Heston and Lily Tomlin to the local cake decorator, must be there on time. The 11:45 a.m. rule is made so the producer, director and crew can concentrate on production and can count on the fact that no last-minute changes will be necessary.

When a guest has not arrived, the producer has less than 15 mintues to pull out a "back-up" tape interview, write new lead-ins, alert the host and the director, get the material to the tape room and still keep the show on schedule.

Our "11:45 rule" was created out of need. We had scheduled Tova Borgnine, creator of a cosmetic catalogue and wife of actor Ernest Borgnine, for a guest appearance. She had not arrived at 12:00! We called another station where she had appeared. She had left in her limo, never to appear at our station. It created a frantic time in the frantic world of live TV.

Sophia Loren visually promotes her glasses at a gala at Atlanta's High Museum during a TV interview.

If the show is not live, arrival time is no less important. Taping times are stringently appointed. Shows often tape 2 or 3 programs in one day using the same audience. They allot 2 hours to tape a 1-hour show, which includes setting up, lighting, sound checks, retakes, etc. Many people are involved. If you are there, it is one less element to worry about.

If you're going to be even 10 minutes late, *Call*!!!

When you arrive, announce yourself to the receptionist. She will call the producer. If the show you are to appear on is live, it is advisable to give her a business card with a contact number and a word or two about what you or your company does in case there are calls from viewers. Make sure the message is clear. "Partners in Crime: Michael Kinsler" is not clear. It could be a detective agency. "Partners in Crime: Handpainted Clothing by Michael Kinsler" is clear.

The TV station, especially at the local level, has a relationship with thousands of people. If your address and phone number are shown on the screen, there may be hundreds of viewers who didn't get a pencil in time and will call for the information.

The owner of Plus Models appeared on our show. She mentioned not having enough large models to fill her assignments. On that day and for months afterwards, the station received hundreds of calls for information. Having the address at the switchboard made it easier to handle viewers' queries. She received 500 applications after her appearance.

In 10 years of television we have dealt with hundreds of guests from Christie Brinkley to Tony Randall,

Your Media Moment

When You Arrive

Be Pleasant

97

The crew can make a difference.
Cameraman Gordon Green's
talent and hospitality provide a
welcoming environment for
guests.

Rosalyn Carter, and Alex Hailey, who were charming. Only 2 guests have been unpleasant. Amazing! All of the others were pleasant, cooperative and undemanding. So many who come through the station seem to realize that everyone working at every level is doing a job. Most guests are respectful of this and treat station employees like professionals.

Pay up Front

It is wonderful to get compliments on the show, and they are appreciated. It is smart to pass on comments and compliments you have heard or seen about the show to the host and even the producer ahead of time. It gives a person a lift to hear good news, and you will be the beneficiary of that good feeling.

Don't overbook if you are touring. Media appearances are fatiguing, and you won't be able to compliment or concentrate if you are exhausted.

While You Wait

Most shows have the traditional "green room." It is a waiting area that may be neither green nor a room, but it is a place for guests to relax prior to their appearance. Some stations have more available space than others.

Just before your appearance, you can expect to be briefed and reminded to keep your comments short and to the point. Pat Mitchell, producer on the Donahue show, says it best. "I tell guests that their answers should be as brief and succinct as possible. They should come to their point and then talk around that point. If they're making a long introductory statement before they really say what they want to say, the audience as well as the host will be asleep by the time they get to the point."

Cosmopolitan *editor Helen Gurley Brown doesn't "wing it." She plans every aspect of her appearance on the "Tonight Show" with Johnny Carson.*

These are some of the things you should be aware of but may not be told during the briefing.

Remember:

1. Be enthusiastic, energetic and caring about your subject.
2. According to communications research, 55 percent of the effect you have on people comes from the way you use your face and body, 37 percent from your voice, and only 8 percent is the result of what you say. Translated that means that people look more than they listen. They like to get a message from people who are animated and friendly.
3. If the program is a daytime show, remember most of your professional peers are at the office. You are talking to potential clients, customers or donors. Don't try to impress them. Try to befriend them.
4. Not only do the cameras seem to wash out color from your face, they also seems to take away some energy from your personality. Therefore, it is important to be more animated than usual. Try to create a sense of energy in your voice and mannerisms. Sit forward, speak distinctly and use a strong tone of voice.

During the briefing, check the pronunciation and spelling of your name. Check the title used under your name if it will appear on the screen: "Stephen Marchard, Color Consultant." If the producer is assigned to be with you while you wait, take an interest in his or her job. Ask how she got to the position. You may be establishing a relationship and developing a rapport that will lead to other appearances.

The Studio—
Lights, Camera, Action

A television broadcast studio is wild and wonderful, but beware, it can be distracting. Concentrate on your goal. Don't be distracted from your mission—a good appearance and presentation.

The studio is filled with people and cameras. There are usually 2 or 3 cameras and camerapeople who move around during the show. The director is in the control room, and you rarely see him after the show begins. The floor director is the liaison between the director and the talent. The hand signals the floor director gives are in sight of the host and talent. These signals tell which cameras are on, how much time remains and when the host should get out of the segment.

Most floor directors tell you to look at the host during the interview. Occasionally, you might also be asked to look into the camera. The "active" camera is the one with the bright red light.

Depending on your experience, here are some suggestions on how to proceed:

Stage I. (First-time guest)

A television interview is like a conversation between you and the host. Talk to him and look at him even if he looks away from you to check his notes or look at the floor director.

Stage II. (Accomplished TV guest)

A television interview is like a 3-way conversation between you, the host and the camera or your "friend at home." Look at the host when he speaks to you. Answer to him and from time to time look at your friend "the camera."

Stage III. (Guest who takes phone-in questions)

If you are on a show that takes phone-in questions, look into the camera and listen to the "friend" as the question is asked, then answer the question by looking at the camera (the viewer) and the host.

Your Media Moment

The Camera

The studio is always active. Avoid distractions by concentrating on your host and your subject.

You should always look at the camera so you will have eye contact with the viewer when you are making an offer, giving a sales pitch or making a plea for charity.

Microphones

Technicians in studios or on location shoots use a variety of microphones. There are overhead boom mikes that follow you around, hand-held mikes that you hold like a lollipop just below your mouth or a lavaliere microphone that attaches to your lapel. You may be asked to drop the cord of the lavaliere mike down inside your clothes in order to hide it. When this happens, remember you are "connected." Don't get up suddenly after the interview without disconnecting the mike.

"Two Minutes 'Til Air Time"

When you are seated for the interview, introduce yourself to the host if you haven't met. Don't be shy, you are a PR person for your subject. Pronounce your name for the host and be understanding if he/she is distracted by last-minute instructions or preparations given from the control booth. Sit up tall, lean forward, take 3 deep breaths and think of something funny. This will help to relax you.

Action

Relax. If you have properly prepared your mind, your material and your posture you will do a good job.

Concentrate. There will be distractions—cameras moving, people walking and talking, the interviewer looking away. Focus your attention.

Larry Ashmead, editor of Harper & Row, discussed how to get a book published.

Create Awareness, Not Antagonism

Be energetic. This is your subject. Share it; you care. Your enthusiasm will infect the viewer.

Complications:

1. Be prepared to deal with the unexpected—the host who is reading your information sheets and not listening to your answers, slides that get reversed, videotape that doesn't roll. Cover as best you can and keep going.

2. If the host talks too much, break in at a pause and gracefully make your point, "I agree with what you say, but it is important to remember that _____."

3. If the host gets argumentative, stay cool. It takes two to make an argument, and if you won't "bite," the host will move on. Be positive. Be prepared for the worst possible question. This is a good opportunity to make your strongest point.

4. If the host asks a question and you don't know the answer, admit it. Say, "That is a good question, but I don't know the answer." If the host goes off your subject, answer the question, then say, "Many people ask me _____," and use a bridge to get back on track and make your next point.

Television talk shows are a trade-off. The station gives you free air time in exchange for an entertaining and informative segment. When you are talking about your subject, do it with sincere interest in serving the viewer. TV folks are sensitive to the fine line between advertising and information. Don't get the reputation for being a huckster.

One guest was a particular case in point. He was a charming and interesting man with a rags-to-riches story set in Hollywood.

His media kit was filled with informative and entertaining material about his shop and his clients. The segment was designed to tell how people achieve success in the superstar world, but when he went on the air, the interview became a hard-sell promotion for his products. Every question was answered with a product pitch. The audience and the producer were annoyed at not hearing the kind of story they had been promised. He was a huckster.

On the other hand, when Richard Simmons appeared on our program, he teased, cajoled, and prodded the audience to eat well and be fit and gave hints on how to do it. He informed the viewers about a new concept of exercise programs for the handicapped and about the Broadway musical he had in the works. He gave no plugs for the Anatomy Asylum.

The point of a guest appearance is to create an awareness of a cause, product or service and to tell your story in a newsworthy manner, not to turn program time into a pitch.

When the host begins to wrap up the segment, take this last chance to reinforce your message. Make a brief closing remark thanking the host and repeat the product name.

A compliment or an interesting comment leaves a good impression, especially if you direct it to the host. It also gives you an opportunity to smile, which is a nice way to be remembered.

Your Media Moment

Richard Simmons is an energetic and entertaining guest. He makes fitness and nutrition fun.

The Last Word

Final Instructions

In-Studio

When the segment is over, don't leave immediately. If you have been wearing a mike, it will need to be removed. On a talk show, chat with the host or fellow guests while the credits roll or thank the host while the floor director removes your mike.

On Location

If you are doing an interview on location, the interview is similar but more relaxed. There are opportunities for re-takes if necessary. When the interview is complete, give the camera crew and reporter a chance to check the tape and sound equipment. Even for pros, re-takes are often necessary. Be sure you have all of the supplies and props you might need at hand. Camera crews are usually on a tight schedule and pre-planning is a must.

Curtain Calls

When your TV segment is over, it will seem like the fastest 4 or 40 minutes of your life. It's a bit of a let-down. No matter how the segment went, don't look for curtain calls or bravos from the crew. They are under a great deal of pressure every day to put on a top-notch show and, just like you, they are off looking for an "Atta boy" or "Atta girl" for their part of the show.

Final Follow-through

If your segment isn't a news interview, treats such as cookies, hard candy or samples of your product are a nice way of saying thanks to the crew. They are always enthusiastic about "munchies." You'd think people in TV only get one meal a month.

If you expect an immediate response to a live interview, leave follow-up telephone numbers, addresses or information with the producer or switchboard operator. This can be an appreciated timesaver in a busy industry.

If you receive a good response from your TV appearance, let your contact at the station know about it. The media's job is to inform the public, and a good response to any segment is an indication that they are doing a good job.

Notes get noticed. Notes to key people always show thoughtfulness and good follow-through. Be sure to mention your particular segment. Notes to reporters, hosts or producers can also mention by name crew members who might have been especially helpful or kind to you.

A note to the general manager is also a good idea and one that does the most for the TV personnel with whom you worked. As an outsider, you represent the public, and TV is always interested in developing good relations with the public. A note about the good work his staff did on your behalf or a word about the response that was generated from your appearance will be a gift to him, even better than "munchies."

Bump: From Boston to Seattle...
The producers tell it like it is...
Stay tuned.

Your Media Moment

Tony Randall promotes Minolta copiers on TV. His "Odd Couple" partner Jack Klugman is a spokesman for a rival copier.

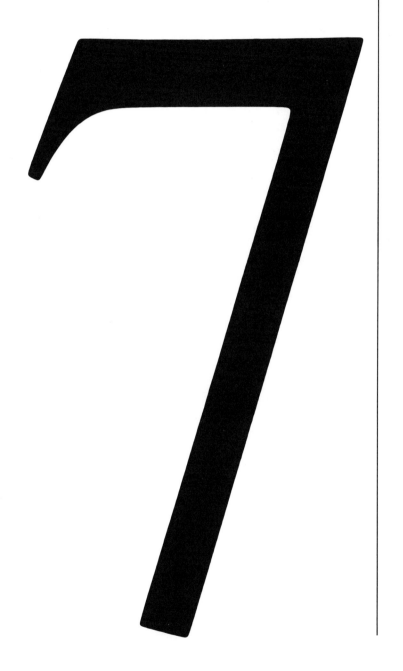

**Talk Show
Producers Talk**

*Wicke laughed with Red Skelton
and Spring was set to tap with
Tommy Tune. Sixty to 70 celebrities appear yearly, but
"Noonday" needs over 500 other
guests. Your place is waiting.*

From "Good Morning America" to "Late Night with Letterman," there's a place for your TV/PR.

There are thousands of talk shows, public affairs programs and newscasts with hundreds of hours of air time to fill. Most talk shows have at least 2 guests a day, 5 days a week, 52 weeks a year, including Christmas and the producer's birthday. Five hundred guests per show multipled by the number of shows on the air certainly leaves time for you. In exchange, you must be entertaining, informative and ready to share some of the how's, why's and wow's of your idea, product or experience.

Each show—talk, public affairs or newscast—has a unique style. Some programs have studio audiences, others discuss one theme throughout the entire show and others, like "Good Morning America," "The Today Show" or the "CBS Morning News," mix their segments. Some segments are as short as 4 minutes while others last for an entire hour show. Producers know their viewers and choose segments that will have the strongest appeal to them in order to score high points in the ever-present ratings wars.

What are the Producer's Needs?

What appeals to producers? What are they looking for? What do talk show producers say when they talk about their needs? When we wrote a 1985 article for *Publisher's Weekly,* the "bible" of the publishing industry, producers made these points:

Television is personality journalism. All producers interviewed agreed *they want good TV personalities, guests or authors who have "energy."* As Carol Chouinard, coordinating producer for "Hour

111

"Hour Magazine" producer Carol Chouinard wants a guest who can sell his/her subject.

Magazine," said, "I want someone who is articulate and can sell his or her subject. We might be so-so on a subject, but if the publicist or guest can present the material in an entertaining or informative way, we are more inclined to go with it."

Gail Steinberg, senior producer of the Donahue show, likes "guests who are articulate, who speak quickly and succinctly and who are aggressive about selling their points." Like other producers whose shows rely heavily on audience participation, she likes "subjects that the audience can chew on, ones they can get involved with because they hold many different opinions on the subject."Dr. Dan Kiley's book, *The Peter Pan Syndrome; Men Who Have Never Grown Up*, was a good example. Guests included a woman married to a man with the Peter Pan traits, a man who declared he had these traits, and the author. The audience related as wives, mothers or men who saw the pattern in their own lives. Calls came from girlfriends, men, and women who saw this pattern in their own choice of men. Many callers affirmed the situation, others denied it. It was lively."

Paul Kelvyn, producer of "Pittsburgh Today," likes "valid information supported by true-life examples and stories." John Marshall, senior producer of Detroit's "Kelly & Company," likes subjects that "everyone has an opinion on and guests who are comfortable and not afraid to talk or express their opinion." Kim Storer, assistant producer of "A.M. Philadelphia," said, "If we're giving a guest that much free promotion time, they must provide something that will make an impact on our audience."

Producers all agreed *a good guest shares information but doesn't hawk it.* Burt Dubrow, executive producer of the syndicated "Sally Jesse Raphael Show," says, "I don't like it when a guest makes a plug for a book or a product. Examples and specific tips whet the appetite for more information, and that's what makes sales.''

It is a well-known fact in the TV industry that guests who make a hard pitch for any product or service on the air are not likely ever to see the light of that producer's air time again.

Because personality rather than subject matter is often the deciding point in booking a guest, Betsy Alexander, senior producer for "A.M. Cleveland," adds, "There are services to train people to do a better job on television. This may be a good investment in learning how to become more relaxed and better TV."

Not only is personality important in getting a guest booked, so are the "hooks" and "angles" that help a producer determine how to make a segment good for television. *Producers want to be timely.* Jane Stoddard, executive producer of Washington's "Panorama," looks at "what is going on in the world" before choosing her guests. Kim Storer of "A.M. Philadelphia" comments, "What's going on in the news is an important part of our show." Timely news hooks make a difference. They save producers time and give the segment impact.

Timing is also critical. "Summers are deadly," says associate producer Crystals Johns of Boston's "Good Day." "May and October are big rating periods," adds Betsy Alexander, "and we go after the guests we want then." If you have a tough time getting booked, take heed. Time your call to fill a producer's need.

Producers also like plenty of lead time and good, pertinent press material. Most producers like at least 3 weeks

Talk Show Producers Talk

Timing and Trends

lead time, particularly producers of theme talk shows who like to schedule additional guests to augment and enliven a certain subject.

Media Kits and Visuals

Make your media kit make a difference. "Many shows make the decision to book a guest based on the materials sent in the press kit without talking on the phone. When the call does come, the decision has already been made," said John Marshall. Seattle's "Good Company" producer Lester Grey adds, "The longer you have to consider a subject, the more likely you're going to be able to find the angles and figure out how you're going to be able to use it."

Producers like reviews, magazine and newspaper articles, human-interest information, and background materials relating to the subject. Whether an author or guest has appeared on the major network shows or not before beginning a national tour, a local producer like Jane Stoddard wants fresh, human-interest information on that guest when he/she appears on "Panorama." She "wants to see a side we haven't seen before and information that helps us bring out the little links between the guest and the viewer." All producers agree that *the less time they have, the more information they need to make the most out of the subject.*

National as well as local producers agree that *visuals count!* As "CBS Morning News" senior producer Roberta Dougherty said, "Television is a visual medium, not just a talk medium." Kelly & Company's John Marshall adds, "We have enough talking heads, we don't need more. Visuals strengthen the audience's understanding of a subject." Television stations across the country are sprucing up their formats, and all producers want visuals, slides, pictures, videotapes or demonstrations to enhance their show. They agree that they are grabbers which attract a viewer's attention.

Television shows are very diverse, and they have different needs. Producers have developed formats that work for them, and *they like ideas tailored to their needs.* Seattle's "Good Company" producer says, "It doesn't take much to find out what works where." Roberta Dougherty of "CBS Morning News," along with other producers, adds, "People should think about segments from a producers point of view. . .how they will work on TV." Publicists, both professional and novice, can then be much more convincing when they say, "I know this is going to be great for your show."

Does TV Sell?

"In the case of first novelist Bret Easton Ellis's book *Less Than Zero,* we could actually track the results of a TV appearance," says Julia Knickerbocker, Simon and Schuster's Vice-President of Publicity. "After Bret appeared on 'The Today Show,' the phones at Simon & Schuster started ringing with requests for media appearances, including 'Firing Line,' a resource we had not considered. Sometimes when an author appears on TV, there is not even a 'blip.'

"There are two factors that help to move a book. First, the host's interest in the book. Bryant Gumbel had read the book and talked enthusiastically with the author. The second is the ability of the author to entice the viewer. Everything worked on this TV appearance, and *Less Than Zero* has since made the Best Seller List."

How Do Producers Make Their Selection?

"Today Show" book producer Emily Boxer sums it up best: "If you're going to deal with ideas, you have to deal

Chambers and Asher on the set.

116

with books, and the books we use have to *make news, be informative or entertain.*"

The same thought applies to selling yourself, your product, your service on TV.

Most television producers sign-off their programs with a tempting list of tomorrow's guests and the promise "of an even more exciting show next time."

We sign-off with an invitation for you to *be* part of the next exciting show on television. If you have an interesting, newsworthy idea, product or service, it's up to you to promote it on television. If you can make the viewer's life easier, more productive, healthier, more attractive, richer, or better and if you are an entertaining and informative personality or have a spokesperson with the right personality for your information, you should launch a plan right now to get your message to TV.

USA Today maintains 75 percent of the information in newspapers is generated by public relations. Television will soon carry similar statistics. As Edward L. Bernays, the 93-year-old father of PR, said, "All public relations must be in the public interest." Products and services must be packaged as news and information, not merely as press-agentry flackery or hype. TV/PR is in the present and the future. . . and *you* can be part of that future.

Talk Show Producers Talk

Sign-Off

Credits

Book Design	Creative Services, Inc.
	Tom Wood
Pictures	Steve Traves-Star Photography
	Tom Asher
	USA Today
	NBC
Copy Editors	Tracy Green
	Ann Woodall
Typesetting	Alice Teeter
Layout	Tommy Westbrook
Book Manufacturer	McNaughton & Gunn
Cover Photo	Lowell Bailey

Chambers & Asher

As partners for 16 years, Chambers & Asher have written books for Simon & Schuster, Harper & Row and Golden Press.

They have worked as television producers for over 10 years and have won 6 regional Emmys as well as awards from the National Association of Television Program Executives and the New York Film Festival. They have served as consultants for ABC in children's public service programming.

Wicke Chambers

A native of Atlanta, Ga., Wicke graduated from the University of Georgia. She and her husband Rufus, an attorney, live in Atlanta with children Rufus Jr., Margaret and Alex.

Spring Asher

Born in Hartford, Conn., Spring attended Cornell University. She and her husband Tom, a stockbroker, live in Atlanta with their children Joey, Juliet and Hugh.

ORDER FORM

Chase Communications, Inc.
1776 Nancy Creek Bluff N.W.
Atlanta, Georgia 30327
Telephone 404 355-4142

Please send _____ copies of

TV/PR
How to promote yourself,
your product, your service,
or your organization
on Television.

Soft Cover $14.95   Hard Cover $19.95

I understand that I may return any book for full refund
if I am not satisfied.

Name: _____

Address: _____

_____ Zip_____

Shipping: $1.50 for the first book and 25¢ for each
           additional book.

_____ I can't wait 3-4 weeks for Book Rate. I am
           enclosing $2.50 per book for Air Mail.

For orders of 5 or more, subtract 20% from total before
adding shipping costs.

ORDER FORM

Chase Communications, Inc.
1776 Nancy Creek Bluff N.W.
Atlanta, Georgia 30327
Telephone 404 355-4142

Please send _____ copies of

TV/PR
How to promote yourself,
your product, your service,
or your organization
on Television.

Soft Cover $14.95   Hard Cover $19.95

I understand that I may return any book for full refund
if I am not satisfied.

Name: _____

Address: _____

_____ Zip_____

Shipping: $1.50 for the first book and 25¢ for each
            additional book.

_____ I can't wait 3-4 weeks for Book Rate. I am
            enclosing $2.50 per book for Air Mail.

For orders of 5 or more, subtract 20% from total before
adding shipping costs.